Dissenting Electorate

Dissenting Electorate

*Those Who Refuse to Vote
and the Legitimacy of
Their Opposition*

Edited by Carl Watner
with Wendy McElroy

McFarland & Company, Inc., Publishers
Jefferson, North Carolina, and London

ISBN 0-7864-0874-X (softcover : 55# alkaline paper)∞

Library of Congress cataloguing data are available

British Library cataloguing data are available

Manufactured in the United States of America

*McFarland & Company, Inc., Publishers
Box 611, Jefferson, North Carolina 28640
www.mcfarlandpub.com*

To the non-voters of the land,
especially Hans Sherrer
(for suggesting this anthology),

Wendy McElroy
(for being born in Canada),

and
Julie Watner
(for being my wife).

And to Wendell Phillips, abolitionist.

"The position of a non-voter in a land where the ballot
is so much idolized, kindles in every beholder's bosom
something of the warm sympathy which awaits
on the persecuted, carries with it all the weight
of a disinterested testimony to truth, and pricks
each voter's conscience with an uneasy doubt, whether after all
voting is right. There is constantly a Mordecai at the gate."
—Wendell Phillips, *Can Abolitionists Vote & Hold Office
Under the Constitution* (1845)

Contents

Contents

Prologue: "Don't Vote: 20 Practical Reasons"

by John Roscoe and Ned Roscoe

Bagatorials *(New York: A Fireside Book published by Simon & Schuster, 1996), p. 15. The authors are California businessmen (father and son) who publish commentary and editorials on their convenience store shopping bags.*

1. You know the present political system doesn't work. You know it doesn't make a difference who wins. It won't make a difference who wins. It won't make a difference to you.

2. You don't believe the majority is always right. Your parents told you the truth when they said they didn't care what the other kids did, you ought to do what's right on your own.

3. You think the government has your name on enough pieces of paper.

4. You don't want to give any candidate the idea that he or she represents you.

5. You think all candidates are lying.

6. You believe you are victimized by politics and politicians. You don't want to give the sanction of the victim to any politician.

7. You think it's immoral to impose your view on others. You believe the best course of action will be decided by individuals without government interference.

8. You think the candidates would say anything, promise anything, and do anything to get elected.

9. You believe power corrupts and absolute power corrupts absolutely. You believe incumbent politicians attain absolute power.

10. You want to send a message to politicians that government isn't the most important thing in your life and you are not going to waste your time voting.

11. You have something better to do with your time.

12. You want to join the 75 percent of American adults who won't vote for the next President of the United States.

13. You don't think political parties represent ideologies. You think the parties are a collection of people who combine to attain power over others.

14. You don't have an intelligent or logical reason to vote. You prefer to act in ways that make sense to you.

15. You know the incumbent almost always wins. You don't think it's in your best interest to add to the power of politicians.

16. You don't believe in the Civic Religion. You don't worship this way.

17. You didn't register. You want to avoid jury duty.

18. You don't believe what they told you in high school Civics. The system doesn't work as they said it would. Since they were wrong about the system, they were almost certainly wrong about the good voting does.

19. You don't want to give government any reason to get bigger, or to legitimize it. You think the 44 percent of the Gross National Product they now spend is enough.

20. You think nonvoting makes a bigger statement than voting.

Introduction

by Carl Watner

I must make a confession: Never in my life have I registered to vote, much less voted, in a political election. Since the time I was a young adult, I had an intuitive feeling that there was something wrong and improper about political voting. In the early 1980s, this book's co-editor, Wendy McElroy, observed that I was not alone. She said there were literally millions upon millions of non-voters. Among them were some who had written about and published their reasons for "refusing to vote." This book is a collection of those writings.

Although there are religious groups, such as the Quakers and Amish, who from the very earliest days of the United States eschewed politics, this chronological collection of essays begins with one written by Adin Ballou, a leading abolitionist and pacifist of the mid–19th century. The attitude of the non-voting abolitionists was that if the American government upheld slavery, then the abolitionists, by not voting, would refuse to sanction and participate in an unjust political system.

With the exception of the second article, which is written by the well-known English philosopher Herbert Spencer, all the remainder of the pieces in this anthology were written by Americans. They were selected because they illustrate a variety of reasons for not voting.

The primary purpose of this book is to prove that there is more to non-voting than one's gut reaction not to participate. *There are very important moral and political reasons for not voting.*

The secondary purpose is to offer an intellectual defense of the non-voter. Non-voters have always been, and actually still are, the majority in most political elections in this country. Their right to remain unrepresented and unsullied by politics ought to be recognized. The fact is that *the non-voters have won every presidential election ever held in this country.*

Political voting is something *sui generis* (something peculiar; something unique) because the institution to which it applies—the state—is different from any other organization in society. Membership (i.e., citizenship) in the state "organization" is compulsory. The state establishes a monopoly of defense services (police, courts, and law) in a given geographic area. Furthermore, it collects its revenues via compulsory levies, euphemistically known as taxation. All those who refuse to acknowledge its jurisdiction or pay its assessments are thrown in jail, have their property confiscated, or both. There is no way to opt out!

Most modern states provide for political elections in which their citizens choose from a slate of predetermined candidates or policies. Majority rule usually determines the outcome. Regardless of the number of people voting, the candidate with the greatest number of votes wins. Even if you don't vote, you are bound by the outcome of the political election. It is still *your* president, *your* representative, *your* tax—even if you haven't voted or voted against the person who won the election.

The main thrust of this book may be summarized in the following points:

1. Voting does not override individual rights or establish the truth. Majorities cannot vote away the rights of minorities.

2. Voting is implicitly a coercive act because it lends support to a compulsory state.

3. Voting reinforces the legitimacy of the state because the participation of voters makes it appear that they approve of the state.

4. There are nonpolitical methods that rely on the spirit of voluntaryism that better serve society.

"Well," one might ask, "if the non-voters are right in not voting, what should we do? Isn't non-voting really a do-nothing tactic?" It might be, except that there are plenty of things we can do if we focus upon ourselves, rather than society as a whole. We are only responsible for ourselves (and our children until they become adults). We can never reform another person. In fact, the only thing within the power of any non-voter "is to present society with one improved unit." As Albert Jay Nock put it, "[A]ges of experience testify that the only way society can be improved is by the individualist method...; that is the method of each 'one' doing his very best" to cultivate his own garden. This is the quiet or patient way of changing society because it concentrates upon bettering the character of men and women as individuals. As the individual units change, the improvement in society will take care of itself. In other words, if one takes care of the means, the end will take care of itself.

Data: Non-Voting Americans

For figures 1976 and earlier, see p. 23 of Charles E. Johnson, Jr., Non-Voting Americans *(Current Population Reports: Special Studies: P-23; no. 102, issued May 1980 by Supt. of Docs. no.: C3.186:P-23/102). For figures after 1976, see* Statistical Abstract of the United States: 1998, *Table No. 458 (p. 279) and Table No. 485 (p. 297).*

Please refer to the bar graph on page 6. The table on this page displays the same data, namely, the actual numbers (rounded off to the hundred-thousands place) of people voting for the winning presidential candidate (after universal suffrage) and the actual number of non-voters (rounded off).

Election year & winning candidate	Voted for winning candidate (numbers in thousands)	Non-voters
1920, Harding	16,143	36,240
1924, Coolidge	15,718	37,328
1928, Hoover	21,392	34,373
1932, Roosevelt	22,810	36,036
1936, Roosevelt	27,753	34,531
1940, Roosevelt	27,308	34,828
1944, Roosevelt	25,607	37,677
1948, Truman	24,179	46,779
1952, Eisenhower	33,936	38,378
1956, Eisenhower	35,590	42,488
1960, Kennedy	34,227	40,834
1964, Johnson	43,130	43,445
1968, Nixon	31,785	47,073
1972, Nixon	47,170	62,443
1976, Carter	40,831	68,524
1980, Reagan	43,904	77,430
1984, Reagan	54,455	81,342
1988, Bush	48,886	90,361
1992, Clinton	44,909	85,099
1996, Clinton	47,402	100,229

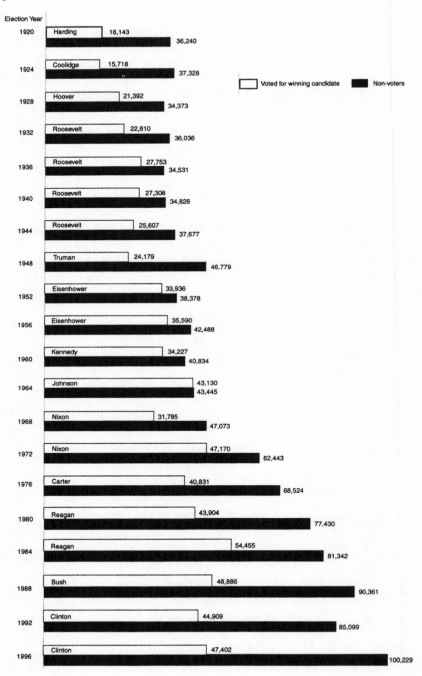

Election Year

1920	Harding	16,143	
			36,240
1924	Coolidge	15,718	
			37,328
1928	Hoover	21,392	
			34,373
1932	Roosevelt	22,810	
			36,036
1936	Roosevelt	27,753	
			34,531
1940	Roosevelt	27,308	
			34,828
1944	Roosevelt	25,607	
			37,677
1948	Truman	24,179	
			46,779
1952	Eisenhower	33,936	
			38,378
1956	Eisenhower	35,590	
			42,488
1960	Kennedy	34,227	
			40,834
1964	Johnson	43,130	
			43,445
1968	Nixon	31,785	
			47,073
1972	Nixon	47,170	
			62,443
1976	Carter	40,831	
			68,524
1980	Reagan	43,904	
			77,430
1984	Reagan	54,455	
			81,342
1988	Bush	48,886	
			90,361
1992	Clinton	44,909	
			85,099
1996	Clinton	47,402	
			100,229

☐ Voted for winning candidate   ■ Non-voters

1

The Superiority of Moral Power Over Political Power

by Adin Ballou

Anti-Slavery Bugle *of New Lisbon, Ohio, June 20, 1845, page 1, photocopy in editor's possession. Adin Ballou (1803-1890) was an American clergyman, pacifist, abolitionist, and president (1841-1851) of the utopian community, Hopedale.*

What is *moral power?* The power which operates on the affections, passions, reason, and moral sentiment of mankind, and thereby *controls* them without *physical force.* It comprehends every description of influence, which, without *applying or threatening* to apply *physical coercion*, tends to determine the *will, conduct* and character of human beings.

What is *political power?* The power of the *State, body politic,* or *civil government*, operating under the forms of law, and *compelling or threatening* to compel subjection to its requirements by *physical force.* It comprehends every description of influence founded on the authority of the *State* which either *applies or threatens* to apply *physical coercion.*

Taking these *two powers,* as they exist in this country, and as they are available to philanthropists and moral reformers, let us *contrast* them. We affirm that moral power is superior.

1. *In respect to their general objects.*

It is the object of moral power to regenerate public sentiment—to superinduce a right *public opinion* and WILL in the great mass of the people. It is the object of political power to *overawe* and *coerce* by *penal laws*, delinquent and refractory *individuals.*—Moral power converts the majority to righteousness in spite of ten thousand difficulties. Political power expresses the new public will in the form of *laws*, and by physical force, *applied* or *threatened*, overawes the minority and coerces the unwilling few into apparent subjection. Moral power does ninety-nine one-hun-

7

dredths of the work, and political power, in its official robes, with a half-unsheathed sword at its side, follows after, claiming all the credit. Which is superior?

2. *In respect to the numbers who exercise them, moral power is superior.*

Moral power is exercised by every human being, in a greater or lesser degree, and is reflected from every created thing. It is vested in the patriarch and the new born babe; in the prince and the beggar; in the philosopher and the idiot.... Moral power is everywhere, in all things. It is exercised by, or at least reflected from, the innumerable hosts of human nature.

But political power is exercised by only a handful of human beings. It is vested, nominally, in the voting citizens, and exercised by their chosen representatives in the several departments of government. And who are the voting citizens? Exclude all females, all minors under twenty-one years of age, all paupers and persons under guardianship, all slaves, all unnaturalized foreigners, and many others for want of the requisite property qualification. The residue will be voting citizens, amounting to less than ONE FOURTH of the whole nation. Deduct from these the sick, helpless, indifferent, and scrupulously conscientious against voting, and the average proportion of actual voters to the mass, will be as one to six, or more likely, as one to ten. Of these, there must be a majority to determine any important issue. The party constituting the majority furnishes nearly all the offices of government, and is itself managed in all its principal doings by a subtle few behind the curtain. The whole political power in this country is virtually in the hands of less than one fiftieth part of the people. A bushel of wheat in a mountain of straw and chaff.

3. *In respect to the prominent details of their operation, moral power is superior.*

Moral power unites male and female in marriage, multiplies human beings, subdues the earth, increases wealth, forms neighborhoods, and builds cities. Political power takes the census, levies taxes, trains soldiers to do its fighting, and assumes the office of protecting the people. Moral power educates the people, intellectually, religiously, morally, socially, and industrially. Political power tickles their ambition, uses up their faculties, consumes their substance, and punishes a few of their grosser crimes....

4. *In respect to their instrumentalities, moral power is superior.*

Look at the number and efficiency of those influences which moral power is every where employing to enlighten and improve mankind. Though many of them are sadly perverted, and need to be rightly directed, yet from their peculiar nature, endless variety, and universal activity, they are capable of producing stupendous results. There is Religion.... Next comes education ... and literature ... and the *influence of woman*.... Such are the instrumentalities of moral power.... In the face of all this, let political power look up and present its vaunted resources: Oh! Its swords, its muskets, its cannons, its powder and ball, ... its prisons; ... its courts; ... its congresses, ...! all crying like the daughters of the horse leech, give! give! office and salary! Mighty, as the political power is, in physical force and money; terrible as it is sometimes in vengeance, what is it compared to moral power?...

5. *In respect to priority and independence of action moral power is superior.*

Moral power is natural, spontaneous, and independent in its action. It originates ideas, feelings, sentiments and *changes* of human conduct. It not only operates *without* but *against* political power; and obliges political power to conform to its dictates. As an illustration, look at the rise and triumph of the Christian religion. It had no political power. It was a babe in a manger. Political power slew fourteen thousand innocents to make sure of its destruction. But it survived and grew up to maturity.... What important change was ever brought about for the public good by political power alone? It originates no such changes. It never thinks of making any such changes, till moral power has suggested them, and prepared the public mind to acquiesce in them! Political power is *artificial, mechanical*, and incapable of doing anything good, without the creative, preparative, and sustaining influence of moral power.

6. *In respect to their freedom and elasticity moral power is superior.*

Moral power is not restricted to times, plans [?], and set forms. It is not confined to certain classes of persons, within certain lines of latitude and longitude, nor to particular cases of conduct and character.... It is at home everywhere, among all human beings, at all times and places. Not so with political power. It is restricted on every side by Constitutions, laws, regulations, precedents, formalities, and usages....

7. *In serious other respects moral power is superior.*

Moral power operates through all its multiform processes, and accomplishes its magnificent results with little show, and at its *own expense*. Political power puts on its robes, sounds a trumpet, and parades its machinery before the public eye, at the expense of the public. It taxes them as heavily as they will bear, compels them to pay ..., and takes care to secure to itself an ample remuneration.... They who are fortunate enough to keep clear of political power are fortunate indeed.

Again. Moral power, being unostentatious and disinterested, exerts a purifying and ennobling influence on the character of its votaries.... But political power has the contrary tendency. It generally renders its devotees more selfish, corrupt, hollow-hearted and tyrannical. Many a decently good man has gone into the labyrinth of politics, and held office to his own moral ruin. And where is there one that ever came out more fit for the kingdom of heaven; unless driven by disgust from its sorceries? It requires no ordinary virtue to maintain one's moral integrity against the seductions of political power.

Finally. Moral power has devised and accomplished nearly all the good that has been done among mankind since the foundation of the world. It has discovered, invented, and perfected, all manner of improvements—mechanical, chemical, intellectual, social, moral and religious.... It has done most of these mighty works in poverty and solitude, with little or no countenance from political power or its worshippers, and not unfrequently in spite of their most deadly opposition. On the other hand, political power seldom patronizes the benefactors of their race till they are quite able to take care of themselves. It generally starves, crucifies, or stones them, and afterwards erects monuments to their memories....

2

The Non-Voter's Right to Ignore the State

by Herbert Spencer

Social Statics *(New York: Robert Schalkenbach Foundation, 1954), p. 190. Originally published in 1850, this excerpt is taken from Part III, Chapter 19, Section 5. Herbert Spencer (1820–1903) was an English philosopher.*

The radicals of our day yet unwittingly profess their belief in a maxim which obviously embodies this doctrine. Do we not continually hear them quote [Sir William] Blackstone's assertion that "no subject of England can be constrained to pay any aids or taxes even for the defense of the realm or the support of government, but such as are imposed by his own consent, or that of his representative in parliament?" And what does this mean? It means, say they, that every man should have a vote. True, but it means much more. If there is any sense in words it is a distinct enunciation of the very right now contended for. In affirming that a man may not be taxed unless he has directly or indirectly given his consent, it affirms that he may refuse to be so taxed; and to refuse to be taxed is to cut all connection with the state. Perhaps it will be said that this consent is not a specific, but a general one, and that the citizen is understood to have assented to everything his representative may do when he voted for him. But suppose he did not vote for him, and on the contrary did all in his power to get elected someone holding opposite views—what then? The reply will probably be that, by taking part in such an election, he tacitly agreed to abide by the decision of the majority. And how if he did not vote at all? Why, then he cannot justly complain of any tax, seeing that he made no protest against its imposition. So, curiously enough, it seems that he gave his consent in whatever way he acted—whether he said yes, whether he said no, or whether he remained neuter! A rather awkward doctrine, this. Here stands an unfortunate citizen who is asked if he will pay money for a certain proffered advantage; and whether he employs the only means of expressing his refusal or does not employ it, we are told that he practically agrees, if only the number of others who agree is greater than the number of those who dissent. And thus we are introduced to the novel principle that A's consent to a thing is not determined by what A says, but by what B may happen to say!

It is for those who quote Blackstone to choose between this absurdity and the doctrine above set forth. Either his maxim implies the right to ignore the state, or it is sheer nonsense.

3

Of Voting

by Lysander Spooner

No Treason: The Constitution of No Authority and a Letter to Thomas F. Bayard, *Larkspur: Pine Tress Press, 1966, pp. 11–16. Originally published in 1870 as* No Treason, No. 6. *This excerpt is taken from Section II. Lysander Spooner (1808–1887) was a Massachusetts lawyer, abolitionist, and radical individualist.*

All the voting that has ever taken place under the Constitution, has been of such a kind that it not only did not pledge the whole people to support the Constitution, but it did not even pledge any one of them to do so, as the following considerations show.

1. In the very nature of things, the act of voting could bind nobody but the actual voters. But owing to the property qualifications required, it is probable that, during the first twenty or thirty years under the Constitution, not more than one-tenth, fifteenth, or perhaps twentieth of the whole population (black and white men, women, and minors) were permitted to vote. Consequently, so far as voting was concerned, not more than one-tenth, fifteenth, or twentieth of those then existing, could have incurred any obligation to support the Constitution.[1]

At the present time,[2] it is probable that not more than one-sixth of the whole population are permitted to vote. Consequently, so far as voting is concerned, the other five-sixths can have given no pledge that they will support the Constitution.

2. Of the one-sixth that are permitted to vote, probably not more than two-thirds (about one-ninth of the whole population) have usually

[1] *In the presidential election of 1824, the first in American history for which there are reliable tabulations of popular votes, barely 350,000 votes were cast at a time when the population was approximately 11,000,000 (the figure for the decennial census of 1820 was 9,638,453; that of 1830 was 12,866,020).*

[2] *In the 1868 election, which occurred just before Spooner was writing, a total of about 5,700,000 votes were cast for the candidates, Gen. Ulysses S. Grant and Horatio Seymour; the population figure for the 1870 census was nearly 40,000,000.*

voted. Many never vote at all. Many vote only once in two, three, five, or ten years, in periods of great excitement.

No one, by voting, can be said to pledge himself for any longer period than that for which he votes. If, for example, I vote for an officer who is to hold his office for only a year, I cannot be said to have thereby pledged myself to support the government beyond that term. Therefore, on the ground of actual voting, it probably cannot be said that more than one-ninth or one-eighth, of the whole population are usually under any pledge to support the Constitution.[3]

3. It cannot be said that, by voting, a man pledges himself to support the Constitution, unless the act of voting be a perfectly voluntary one on his part. Yet the act of voting cannot properly be called a voluntary one on the part of any very large number of those who do vote. It is rather a measure of necessity imposed upon them by others, than one of their own choice. On this point I repeat what was said in a former number,[4] viz.:

> In truth, in the case of individuals, their actual voting is not to be taken as proof of consent, *even for the time being.* On the contrary, it is to be considered that, without his consent having even been asked a man finds himself environed by a government that he cannot resist; a government that forces him to pay money, render service, and forego the exercise of many of his natural rights, under peril of weighty punishments. He sees, too, that other men practice this tyranny over him by the use of the ballot. He sees further, that, if he will but use the ballot himself, he has some chance of relieving himself from this tyranny of others, by subjecting them to his own. In short, he finds himself, without his consent, so situated that, if he use the ballot, he may become a master; if he does not use it, he must become a slave. And he has no other alternative than these two. In self-defense, he attempts the former. His case is analogous to that of a man who has been forced into battle, where he must either kill others, or be killed himself. Because, to save his own life in a battle, a man attempts to take the lives of his opponents, it is not to be inferred that the battle is one of his own choosing. Neither in contests with the ballot—which is a mere substitute for a bullet—because, as his only chance of self-preservation, a man uses a ballot, is it to be inferred that the contest is one into which he voluntarily entered; that he voluntarily set up all his own natural rights, as a stake against those of others, to be lost or won by the mere power of numbers. On the contrary, it is to be considered that, in an exigency into which he had been forced by others, and in which no other

---

[3] *Relative percentages of those voting out of the total population have steadily increased since this was written but, in the main, Spooner's conjecture was borne out down until the adoption of the 19th Amendment, which ended sexual discrimination in national elections in 1920. The voters in the elections between 1870 and 1920 varied from one fifth to one eighth of the whole population. In recent years, since 1940, the figure has usually fluctuated between one-third and two-fifths.*

[4] *See* No Treason, *No. 2, pages 5 and 6.*

means of self-defense offered, he, as a matter of necessity, used the only one that was left to him.

Doubtless the most miserable of men, under the most oppressive government in the world, if allowed the ballot, would use it, if they could see any chance of thereby meliorating their condition. But it would not, therefore, be a legitimate inference that the government itself, that crushes them, was one which they had voluntarily set up, or even consented to.

Therefore, a man's voting under the Constitution of the United States, is not to be taken as evidence that he ever freely asserted to the Constitution, *even for the time being*. Consequently we have no proof that any very large portion, even of the actual voters of the United States, ever really and voluntarily consented to the Constitution, *even for the time being*. Nor can we ever have such proof, until every man is left perfectly free to consent, or not, without thereby subjecting himself or his property to be disturbed or injured by others.

As we can have no legal knowledge as to who votes from choice, and who from the necessity thus forced upon him, we can have no legal knowledge, as to any particular individual, that he voted from choice; or, consequently, that by voting, he consented, or pledged himself, to support the government. Legally speaking, therefore, the act of voting utterly fails to pledge *any one* to support the government. It utterly fails to prove that the government rests upon the voluntary support of anybody. On general principles of law and reason, it cannot be said that the government has any voluntary supporters at all, until it can be distinctly shown who its voluntary supporters are.

4. As taxation is made compulsory on all, whether they vote or not, a large proportion of those who vote, no doubt do so to prevent their own money being used against themselves; when, in fact, they would have gladly abstained from voting, if they could thereby have saved themselves from taxation alone, to say nothing of being saved from all the other usurpations and tyrannies of the government. To take a man's property without his consent, and then to infer his consent because he attempts, by voting, to prevent that property from being used to his injury, is a very insufficient proof of his consent to support the Constitution. It is, in fact, no proof at all. And as we can have no legal knowledge as to who the particular individuals are, if there are any, who are willing to be taxed for the sake of voting, we can have no legal knowledge that any particular individual consents to be taxed for the sake of voting; or, consequently, consents to support the Constitution.

5. At nearly all elections, votes are given for various candidates for the same office. Those who vote for the unsuccessful candidates cannot properly be said to have voted to sustain the Constitution. They may,

with more reason, be supposed to have voted, not to support the Constitution, but specially to prevent the tyranny which they anticipate the successful candidate intends to practice upon them under color of the Constitution; and therefore may reasonably be supposed to have voted against the Constitution itself. This supposition is the more reasonable, inasmuch as such voting is the only mode allowed to them of expressing their dissent to the Constitution.

6. Many votes are usually given for candidates who have no prospect of success. Those who give such votes may reasonably be supposed to have voted as they did, with a special intention, not to support, but to obstruct the execution of, the Constitution; and therefore, against the Constitution itself.

7. As all the different votes are given secretly (by secret ballot), there is no legal means of knowing, from the votes themselves, who votes for, and who against, the Constitution. Therefore, voting affords no legal evidence that any particular individual supports the Constitution. And where there can be no legal evidence that any particular individual supports the Constitution, it cannot legally be said that anybody supports it. It is clearly impossible to have any legal proof of the intentions of large numbers of men, where there can be no legal proof of the intentions of any particular one of them.

8. There being no legal proof of any man's intentions, in voting, we can only conjecture them. As a conjecture, it is probably, that a very large proportion of those who vote, do so on this principle, viz., that if, by voting, they could but get the government into their own hands (or that of their friends), and use its powers against their opponents, they would then willingly support the Constitution; but if their opponents are to have the power, and use it against them, then they would *not* willingly support the Constitution.

In short, men's voluntary support of the Constitution is doubtless, in most cases, wholly contingent upon the question whether, by means of the Constitution, they can make themselves masters, or are to be made slaves.

Such contingent consent as that is, in law and reason, no consent at all.

9. As everybody who supports the Constitution by voting (if there are any such) does so secretly (by secret ballot), and in a way to avoid all personal responsibility for the act of his agents or representatives, it cannot legally or reasonably be said that anybody at all supports the Constitution by voting. No man can reasonably or legally be said to do such a thing as to assent to, or support, the Constitution, *unless he does it openly,*

and in way to make himself personally responsible for the acts of his agents, so long as they act within the limits of the power he delegates to them.

10. As all voting is secret (by secret ballot), and as all secret governments are necessarily only secret bands of robbers, tyrants, and murderers, the general fact that our government is practically carried on by means of such voting, only proves that there is among us a secret band of robbers, tyrants and murderers, whose purpose is to rob, enslave, and, so far as necessary to accomplish their purposes, murder, the rest of the people. The simple fact of the existence of such a band does nothing towards proving that "the people of the United States," or any one of them, voluntarily supports the Constitution.

For all the reasons that have now been given, voting furnishes no legal evidence as to who the particular individuals are (if there are any), who voluntarily support the Constitution. It therefore furnishes no legal evidence that anybody supports it voluntarily.

So far, therefore, as voting is concerned, the Constitution, legally speaking, has no supporters at all.

And, as matter of fact, there is not the slightest probability that the Constitution has a single bona fide supporter in the country. That is to say, there is not the slightest probability that there is a single man in the country, who both understands what the Constitution really is, *and sincerely supports it for what it really is.*

The ostensible supporters of the Constitution, like the ostensible supporters of most other governments, are made up of three classes, viz.: 1. Knaves, a numerous and active class, who see in the government an instrument which they can use for their own aggrandizement or wealth. 2. Dupes—a large class, no doubt—each of whom, because he is allowed one voice out of millions in deciding what he may do with his own person and his own property, and because he is permitted to have the same voice in robbing, enslaving, and murdering others, that others have in robbing, enslaving, and murdering himself, is stupid enough to imagine that he is a "free man," a "sovereign"; that this is "a free government"; "a government of equal rights," "the best government on earth,"[5] and such like absurdities. 3. A class who have some appreciation of the evils of government, but either do not see how to get rid of them, or do not choose to so far sacrifice their private interests as to give themselves seriously and earnestly to the work of making a change.

---

[5] *Suppose it be "the best government on earth," does that prove its own goodness, or only the badness of all other governments?*

4

Against Woman Suffrage

by Lysander Spooner

Benjamin Tucker (editor), Liberty *(Boston: Vol. I, No. 22. June 10, 1882, p. 4). Reprinted in "Radical Periodicals in the United States," Second Series 1881–1961 by Greenwood Reprint Corporation, Westport, Connecticut (1970). This article originally appeared February 24, 1877, in* "New Age, J.M.L. Babcock's journal."

Women are human beings, and consequently have all the natural rights that any human beings can have. They have just as good a right to *make laws* as men have, and no better; AND THAT IS JUST NO RIGHT AT ALL. No human being, nor any number of human beings, have any right to *make laws,* and compel other human beings to obey them. To say that they have is to say that they are the masters and owners of those of whom they require such obedience.

The only law that any human being can rightfully be *compelled* to obey is simply the law of justice. And justice is not a thing that is *made,* or that can be unmade, or altered, by any human authority. It is a *natural* principle, inhering in the very nature of man and of things. It is that natural principle which determines what is mine and what is thine, what is one man's right or property and what is another man's right or property. It is, so to speak, the line that Nature has drawn between one man's rights of person and property and another man's rights of person and property.

But for this line, which Nature has drawn separating the rights of one man from the rights of any and all other men, no human being could be said to have any rights whatever. Every human being would be at the mercy of any and all other human beings who were stronger than he.

This natural principle, which we will call justice, and which assigns to each and every human being his or her rights, and separates them from the rights of each and every other human being, is, I repeat, not a thing that man has *made,* but is a matter of science to be learned, like mathematics, or chemistry, or geology. And all the *laws,* so called, that men have ever *made*, either to create, define, or control the rights of individuals, were intrinsically just as absurd and ridiculous as would be laws to create, define, or control mathematics, or chemistry, or geology.

Substantially all the tyranny and robbery and crime that governments have ever committed—and they have either themselves committed, or licensed others to commit, nearly all that have ever been committed in the world by anybody—have been committed by them under the pretense of *making laws.* Some man, or some body of men, have claimed the right, or usurped the power, of *making laws,* and compelling other men to obey; thus setting up their own will, and enforcing it, in place of that natural law, or natural principle, which says that no man or body of men can rightfully exercise any arbitrary power whatever over the persons or property of other men.

There are a large class of men who are so rapacious that they desire to appropriate to their own uses the persons and properties of other men. They combine for the purpose, call themselves governments, *make what they call laws, and* then employ courts, and governors, and constables, and, in the last resort, bayonets, to enforce obedience.

There is another class of men, who are devoured by ambition, by the love of power, and the love of fame.

They think it is a very glorious thing to rule over men; to make laws to govern them. But as they have no power of their own to compel obedience, they unite with the rapacious class before mentioned, and become their tools. They promise to *make such laws* as the rapacious class desire, if this latter class will but authorize them to act in their name, and furnish the money and the soldiers necessary for carrying their laws, so called, into execution.

Still another class of men, with a sublime conceit of their own wisdom, or virtue, or religion, think they have a right, and a sort of divine authority, for making laws to govern those who, they think, are less wise, or less virtuous, or less religious than themselves. They assume to know what is best for all other men to do and not to do, to be and not to be, to have and not to have. And they conspire to *make laws to compel* all those other men to conform to their will, or, as they would say, to their superior discretion. They seem to have no perception of the truth that each and every human being has had given to him a mind and body of his own, separate and distinct from the minds and bodies of all other men; and that each man's mind and body have, by nature, rights that are utterly separate and distinct from the rights of any and all other men; that these individual rights are really the only *human* rights there are in the world;

that each man's rights are simply the right to control his own soul, and body, and property, according to his own will, pleasure, and discretion, so long as he does not interfere with the equal right of any other man to the free exercise and control of his own soul, body, and property. They seem to have no conception of the truth that, so long as he lets all other men's souls, bodies, and properties alone, he is under no obligation whatever to believe in such wisdom, or virtue, or religion as they do, or as they think best for him.

This body of self-conceited, wise, virtuous, and religious people, not being sufficiently powerful of themselves to *make laws* and enforce them upon the rest of mankind, combine with the rapacious and ambitious classes before mentioned to carry out such purposes as they can all agree upon. And the farce, and jargon, and babel they all make of what they call government would be supremely ludicrous and ridiculous, if it were not the cause of nearly all the poverty, ignorance, vice, crime, and misery there are in the world.

Of this latter class—that is, the self-conceited wise, virtuous, and religious class—are those woman suffrage persons who are so anxious that women should participate in all the falsehood, absurdity, usurpation, and crime *of making laws,* and enforcing them upon other persons. It is astonishing what an amount of wisdom, virtue, and knowledge they propose to inflict upon, or force into, the rest of mankind, if they can but be permitted to participate with the men in *making laws.* According to their own promises and predictions, there will not be a single natural human being left upon the globe, if the women can but get hold of us, and add their power to that of the men in making such laws as nobody has any right to make, and such as nobody will be under the least obligation to obey. According to their programme, we are to be put into their legislative mill, and be run through, ground up, worked over, and made into some shape in which we shall be scarcely recognized as human beings. Assuming to be gods, they propose to make us over into their own image. But there are so many different images among them, that we can have, at most, but one feature after one model, and another after another. What the whole conglomerate human animal will be like, it is impossible to conjecture.

In all conscience, is it not better for us even to bear the nearly unbearable ills inflicted upon us by the laws already made,—at any rate is it not better for us to be (if we can but be permitted to be) such simple human beings as Nature made us,—than suffer ourselves to be made over into such grotesque and horrible shapes as a new set of lawmakers would make us into, if we suffer them to try their powers upon us?

The excuse which the women offer for all the laws which they propose to inflict upon us is that they themselves are oppressed by the laws that now exist. Of course they are oppressed; and so are all *men*—except the oppressors themselves—oppressed by the laws that are *made*. As a general rule, oppression was the only motive for which laws were ever *made*. If men wanted justice, and only justice, no laws would ever need to be *made*; since justice itself is not a thing that can be *made*. If men or women, or men and women, want justice, and only justice, their true course is *not to make any more laws, but to abolish the laws—all the laws— that have already been made*. When they shall have abolished all the laws that have already been *made*, let them give themselves to the study and observance, and, if need be, the enforcement, of that one universal law— the law of Nature—which is "the same at Rome and Athens"—in China and in England—and which *man did not make*. Women and men alike will then have their *rights; all their rights; all the rights that Nature gave them*. But until then, neither men nor women will have anything that they can call their *rights*. They will at most have only such liberties or privileges as the laws that are *made* shall see fit to allow them.

If the women, instead of petitioning to be admitted to a participation in the power of *making more laws*, will but give notice to the present lawmakers that they (the women) are going up to the State House, and are going to throw all the existing statute books in the fire, they will do a very sensible thing,—one of the most sensible things it is in their power to do. And they will have a crowd of men—at least all the sensible and honest men in the country to go with them.

But this subject requires a treatise, and is not to be judged of by the few words here written. Nor is any special odium designed to be cast on the woman suffragists; many of whom are undoubtedly among the best and most honest of all those foolish people who believe that laws should be *made*.

5

Political Methods vs. Nonviolent Resistance

by Francis Tandy

Francis Dashwood Tandy, Voluntary Socialism (Denver: Francis D. Tandy, 1896), pp. 191–201. These excerpts are taken from Chapter XIII, "Methods." Francis Tandy was born in 1867, and lived at least until the second decade of the 20th Century. The purpose of his book was to provide "a brief but lucid outline" of individualist anarchism.

Political methods must be condemned without even these qualifications. The ballot is only a bullet in another form. An appeal to the majority is an appeal to brute force. It is assumed that, since all men are on the average equally able to carry a musket, the side which has the largest number of adherents would probably conquer in case of war. So, instead of actually fighting over questions, it is more economical to count noses and see which side would probably win. The political method is a form of revolution, and most of the arguments directed against the latter are valid when applied to the former. The result shown at the polls indicates a certain stage of mental development in the community. As that mental development is changed, the political manifestations of it change also. So we are brought back to the original starting point. If we wish to effect the abolition of the State through politics, we must first teach people how we can get along without it. When that is done, no political action will be necessary. The people will have outgrown the State and will no longer submit to its tyranny. It may still exist and pass laws, but people will no longer obey them, for its power over them will be broken. Political action can never be successful until it is unnecessary....

Any one who has had any experience in practical politics must know how hopeless it is to attempt to effect any reform—especially any reform in the direction of freedom—by that means. Platforms are adopted to get elected on, not to be carried out in legislation. The real position of a party

22

depends, not upon the justness or unjustness of measures, but upon the probabilities of re-election. Scheming and "diplomacy" are the methods of the candidates for public office. Reasoning and honest conviction do not concern them in the least....

These facts give us a glimpse of the intricacies of politics. How can the reformer or business man who has to earn his living hope to cope with the professional politician while this is the case? The politician is in possession of the field. He is able to devote his whole time to studying the situation and to heading off any move to oust him. What can you do about it? You can give the matter a little attention after business hours and think you grasp the situation. You can vote once a year or so for a different set of thieves. If you are very enterprising you can go to the primaries and think you are spoiling the politician's little game. What do you think the politician has been doing since last election? Instead of going to primaries you might as well go to—another place which politics more nearly resembles than anything on this earth. Perhaps better, for a spook devil would probably be an easier task-master than a politician in flesh and blood. You can do what you please, the politician is dealing from a stacked deck and has the best of the bunco game all the time.

At its very best, an election is merely an attempt to obtain the opinion of the majority upon a given subject, with the intention of making the minority submit to that opinion. This is in itself a radical wrong. The majority has no more right, under Equal Freedom, to compel the majority. When a man votes he submits to the whole business. By the act of casting his ballot, he shows that he wishes to coerce the other side, if he is in the majority. He has, consequently, no cause for complaint if he is coerced himself. He has submitted in advance to the tribunal, he must not protest if the verdict is given against him. If every individual is a sovereign, when he votes he abdicates. Since I deny the right of the majority to interfere in my affairs, it would be absurd for me to vote and thereby submit myself to the will of the majority....

Must we then sit still and let our enemies do as they please? By no means. Three alternatives offer themselves, active resistance, nonviolent resistance and non-resistance. The folly of the first has already been demonstrated. Non-resistance is just as bad. Unless we resist tyranny, we encourage it and become tyrants by tacitly consenting to it. But nonviolent resistance still remains. The most perfect nonviolent resistance has often been practiced by the Quakers. During the Civil War the Quakers all absolutely refused to serve in the army. In European countries they have resisted conscription in the same manner. What could be done about it? A few were imprisoned, but they stood firm, and finally, by nonviolent resistance, they have gained immunity from this particular form of tyranny....

To gain anything by political methods, it is first necessary to gain a majority of the votes cast, and even then you have to trust to the integrity of the men elected to office. But with nonviolent resistance this is unnecessary. A good strong minority is all that is needed. It has been shown that the attitude of the State is merely a crude expression of the general consensus of the opinion of its subjects. In determining this consensus, quality must be taken into consideration as well as quantity. The opinion of one determined and intelligent man may far outweigh that of twenty lukewarm followers of the opposition. "To apply this consideration to practical politics, it may be true that the majority in this country are favorable, say, to universal vaccination. It does not follow that a compulsory law embodies the will of the people; because the very man who is opposed to that law is at least ten times more anxious to gain his end than his adversaries are to gain theirs. He is ready to make far greater sacrifices to attain it. One man rather wishes for what he regards as a slight sanitary safeguard; the other is determined not to submit to a gross violation of his liberty. How differently the two are actuated! One man is willing to pay a farthing in the pound for a desirable object; the other is ready to risk property and perhaps life to defeat that object. In such cases as this it is sheer folly to pretend that counting heads is a fair indication of the forces behind." (Donisthorpe, *Law in a Free State*. London: Macmillan, 1895, pp. 123-124.) A strong, determined and intelligent minority, employing methods of nonviolent resistance, would be able to carry all before it. For the same men, being in a numerical minority, would be powerless to elect a single man to office.

Another thing must be remembered. Nonviolent resistance can never pass a law. It can only nullify laws. Consequently, it can never be used as a means of coercion and is particularly adopted to the attainment of Anarchy. All other schools of reform propose to compel people to do something. For this they must resort to force, usually by passing laws. These laws depend upon political action for their inauguration and physical violence for their enforcement. Anarchists are the only reformers who do not advocate physical violence. Tyranny must ever depend upon the weapon of tyranny, but Freedom can be inaugurated only by means of Freedom.

The first thing that is necessary, to institute the changes outlined in this book, is to convince people of the benefit to be derived from them. This means simply a campaign of education. As converts are gradually gained, nonviolent resistance will grow stronger. At first it must be very slight, but still has its effect. Even the refusal to vote does more than is often supposed. In some States the number of persons who, from lethargy or from principle, refuse to vote is large enough to alarm the politicians. They actually talk at times of compulsory voting. This shows how much even such a small amount of nonviolent resistance is feared. As the cause gains converts and strength, this nonviolent resistance can assume a wider field. The more it is practiced greater attention will be drawn to underlying principles. Thus education and nonviolent resistance go hand in hand and help each other, step by step, towards the goal of human Freedom.

6

On Underwriting an Evil

by Frank Chodorov

Out of Step: The Autobiography of an Individualist *(New York: The Devin-Adair Company, 1962), pp. 36–49. This excerpt appears as Chapter IV. Frank Chodorov (1887–1966) was founding editor of* The Freeman *and associate editor of* Human Events.

I voted for Teddy Roosevelt in 1912. I haven't voted in a presidential election since.

At first it was sheer instinct that dissuaded me from casting my ballot. I listened to the performance promises of the various candidates and the more I listened the more confused I became. They seemed to me to be so contradictory, so vague, so devoid of principle, that I could not bring myself in favor of one or the other. Particularly was I impressed by the candidates' evaluations of one another. Neither one had a good word to say of his opponent, and each was of the opinion that the other fellow was not the kind of man to whom the affairs of state could be safely entrusted. Now, I reasoned, these fellows were politicians, and as such should be better acquainted with their respective qualifications for office than I could be; it was their business to know such things. Therefore, I had to believe candidate A when he said that candidate B was untrustworthy, as I had to believe candidate B when he said the same of candidate A. In the circumstances, how could I vote for either? Judging by their respective evaluations of each other's qualifications I was bound to make the wrong decision whichever way I voted.

I put off voting from one election to another, perhaps hoping that sometime a compelling choice would be offered me. I was, I believe, looking for a candidate who would stand for a philosophy of government, something that would be above the ephemeral. In time it dawned on me that I was being romantic, that with principles—that is, moral or philosophic concepts—politics simply has nothing to do, except as convenient

26

slogans in the promotion of its business, which is the acquisition of power. I soon realized that the art of politics consisted in the balancing of various group interests, one against the other, so as either to attain or retain rulership over all. It was a juggling act.

This is no reflection on the intellectual integrity of the politician. His business does not call for any such quality and his supporters would be outraged if he presumed to bring it into bearing. Assuming that a candidate were a convinced free trader, or believed that veterans do not benefit from handouts, or—to go to an extreme—that the nation's bonded indebtedness is a burden on the economy, it would be political suicide for him to voice such an opinion. A candidate in the North who espoused "white supremacy" would have as little chance as a candidate in the South who did not. Were a considerable segment of the population, sufficiently large to offset the opposition, in favor of putting disabilities on Jews, Catholics or Masons, you would find candidates advocating legislation of that kind even though their private judgment were against it. The politician's opinion is the opinion of his following, and their opinion is shaped by what they believe to be in their own interest.

It was always thus. Even when kings ruled by "divine right," the throne was held in place by the proper juxtaposition of rival and envious nobles. When the ambition of a particular noble got out of hand and an army was needed to make him respect divinity, the money-lenders supplied the war funds and received their compensation, usually a grant of land and the privilege of collecting rent from the users. In the eighteenth century the rising class of manufacturers and merchants came to the support of the king in his quarrels with his nobles, in exchange for tariffs, cartel privileges and the "rights" to foreign exploitation.

Constitutionalism and the extension of the suffrage did not alter the character of politics. These institutions merely increased the number of claimants for special privileges and complicated art of balancing interests. In the early years of our country the politician's problem was quite simple: the pressure groups consisted of tariff-seekers, land-grabbers, money-brokers, franchise-hunters and a few others, and the balancing of interests was fixed by the size of campaign contributions. In due time, thanks to professional organizers, others got into the act, and the politician now has to consider the privilege claims of vote-laden and skillfully led proletarians, farmers, teachers, veterans—a host of articulate "minority" groups—as well as the traditional claimants. The juggling has become more intricate.

That this result was inevitable becomes evident when we consider the nature of the ballot. It is nothing but a fragment of sovereignty. It represents a small piece of the power which, in an absolutism, is vested in a single person or an oligarchy. And, just as the substance of political power consists of castles and food and pleasures for the autocrat, so does the holder of this fragment of diffused sovereignty spell "good times." In short, the right of suffrage carries with it the expectation of economic welfare, and that expectation is still the motive behind the "×" set down along the candidate's name. We vote, in the main, by our belly-interest.

The individual voter learned in time that the minuscule piece of sovereignty he held brought him no profit unless it was augmented by many other pieces, so that the total would be a bargaining power of proportions. Thus came the modern pressure group. It is the business of the leaders of such groups to convince the aspirant for office that their following cannot be ignored with impunity. It is the business of the candidate to weigh the relative voting strength of the various groups and, finding it impossible to please all, to try to buy the strongest with promises. It is a deal. Any moral evaluation of the deal is silly, unless we condemn politics as a whole, for there is no way for the politician to attain power unless he engages in such deals. In a democracy sovereignty lies in the hands of the voters, and it is they who propose the trading.

The vast majority of the voters are outside these pressure groups; there are too many of them, too diversified in their interests to permit of organization. I am one of them. I might vote for one or the other candidate if I belonged to some such pressure group and accepted his promise of improvement of my lot at face value. For instance, if I were a farmer in line for a government handout, I would certainly cast my ballot for the candidate who, in my opinion, could be relied upon to come through when elected, or, if I were a member of a union, I would most assuredly trade my vote for some advantage which the gentleman in question promised to deliver to my organization; provided, of course, that I believed him. But, I belong to no pressure group and am instinctively averse to accepting any advantage over my fellow man. What is more, I am not looking for a job in the bureaucracy, nor is my brother-in-law in line for such a job; nor am I anxious for a government contract and I do not own any land that might by suitable for a post office. That is to say, I cannot profit, directly or indirectly, from the election of either candidate. I am of the great mass of unorganized citizens and, therefore, see no reason for casting my ballot for one or the other.

Admitting that there is no difference in the political philosophies of the contending candidates, should I not choose the "lesser of two evils?"

But, which of the two qualifies? If my man prevails, then those who voted against him are loaded down with the "greater evil," while if my man loses then it is they who have chosen the "lesser evil." Voting for the "lesser of two evils," makes no sense, for it is only a matter of opinion as to which is the lesser. Usually, such a decision is based on prejudice, not on principle. Besides, why should I compromise with evil?

If I were to vote for the "lesser of two evils" I would in fact be subscribing to whatever that "evil" does in office. He could claim a mandate for his official acts, a sort of blank check, with my signature, into which he could enter his performances. My vote is indeed a moral sanction, upon which the official depends for support of his acts, and without which he would feel rather naked. In a democracy the acquiescence of the citizenry is necessary for the operation of the State, and a large vote is a prelude for such acquiescence. Even in a totalitarian state the dictators feel it necessary to hold elections once in a while, just to assure themselves and others of the validity of their rule, though the voting is compulsory and the ballot is one-sided, they can point to the large percentage of the electorate who underwrite their rule. In a free election, even though the difference between the candidates is a matter of personality, or between tweedledee and tweedledum, the successful candidate (though he might be the "lesser of two evils") can similarly maintain that he holds a mandate from the people. It is to the credit of a democracy that I can choose not to vote. I am not compelled to give my moral support to an "evil."

Getting back to the economic advantages that the candidates promise me, in exchange for my vote, my reason tells me that they cannot make good on their promises, except by taking something from my fellow men and delivering it to me. For, government is not a producer. It is simply a social instrument enjoying a monopoly of coercion, which it is supposed to use so as to prevent the indiscriminate use of coercion by individuals on one another. Its purpose in the scheme of things is to protect each of us in the enjoyment of those rights with which we are born. Its competence is in the field of behavior; it can compel us to do what we do not want to do, or to prevent us from doing what we want to do. But, it cannot produce a thing. Therefore, when it undertakes to improve the economy, it is compelled by its own limitations to the taking from one group of citizens and giving to another; it uses its monopoly of coercion for the distribution of wealth. So that, when I vote for the candidate who promises me betterment in my economic condition, I am condoning and encouraging some form of robbery. That does not square with my moral values....

All in all, I see no good reason for voting and have refrained from doing so for about a half century. During that time, my more conscientious compatriots (including, principally, the professional politicians and their ward heelers) have conveniently provided me with presidents and with governments, all of whom have run the political affairs of the country as they should be run—that is, for the benefit of the politicians. They have put the nation into two major wars and a number of minor ones. Regardless of what party was in power, the taxes have increased and so did the size of the bureaucracy. Laws have been passed, a whole library of them, and most of these laws, since they are not self-enforcing, have called for enforcement agencies, who have interminably interpreted the laws which created them and thus have spawned more laws. The effect of these laws is (a) to put restraints on the individual and (b) to concentrate in the hands of the central government all the powers that once were assigned to local government; the states are now little more than administrative units of the national government. Political power has increased, social power has waned. Would it have been different if I had voted? I don't think so.

Statistics indicate that nearly half the electorate—those eligible to vote—do not exercise their privilege. Whether such non-voting is due to apathy or a conscious rejection of the candidates and their philosophies of government (or the lack of any philosophy) it would be difficult to tell. Perhaps the stay-at-homes might be interested in registering their conviction if two candidates stated exactly what they stood for, without equivocation and without offering inducements to various pressure groups; but, in the absence of such an experiment, the best we can say is that a goodly number find no sense in voting.

It is interesting to speculate on what would happen if, say seventy-five percent of the electorate refrained from casting their ballots; more than that is out of the question, for at least a quarter of the voting public are concerned with what they can get for themselves from the election of this or that candidate; their belly-interest is entirely too strong to keep them away from the polls. In the first place, the politicians would not take such a repudiation of their custodianship in good grace. We can take it for granted that they would undertake to make voting compulsory, bringing up the hoary argument that a citizen is morally obligated to do his duty. If military service can be made compulsory why not political service? And so, if three-quarters of the citizenry were to refrain from voting, a fine would be imposed on first offenders and more dire punishment meted out to repeaters. The politician must have the moral support of a goodly number of votes.

Putting aside compulsion, what might be the effect on the citizenry and the social order if an overwhelming majority should quit voting? Such abstinence would be tantamount to giving this notice to politicians: since we as individuals have decided to look after our public affairs, your services are no longer required. Having assumed social power we would, as individuals, have to assume social responsibility. The job of looking after community affairs would devolve on all of us. We might hire an expert to tell us about the most improved fire-fighting apparatus, or a street cleaning manager, or an engineer to build us a bridge; but the final decision, particularly in the matter of raising funds to defray the costs, would rest with the town hall meeting. The hired specialists would have no authority other than that necessary for the performance of their contractual duties; coercive power, which is the essence of political authority, would be exercised, when necessary, by the committee of the whole.

There is some warrant for the belief that the social order would be considerably improved when the individual is responsible for and, therefore, responsive to its needs. He would no longer have the law or the lawmakers to cover his sins of omission or commission. Need for the neighbors' good opinion would be sufficient to induce acceptance of jury duty, and no loopholes in the draft law, no recourse to political pull, would be possible when danger to the community calls him to bear arms in its defense. In his private affairs, the now sovereign individual would have to abide by the dictum of the market place: produce or you will not eat, for no law will help you. In his public behavior he must be decent or suffer the sentence of social ostracism, with no recourse to legal exoneration. From a law-abiding citizen he would be transmuted into a self-respecting man.

Would chaos result? No, there would be order, without law to disturb it. But, let us define chaos of the social kind. Is it not disharmony resulting from social friction? When we trace social friction to its source do we not find that it seminates in a feeling of unwarranted hurt or injustice? Now, when one may take by law that which another man has put his labor into, we have injustice of the keenest kind for the denial of a man's right to possess and enjoy what he produces is akin to a denial of life. Yet the confiscation of property is the first business of government. It is indeed its only business, for the government has no competence for anything else. It cannot produce a single "good" and so must resort to doing the only thing within its province: to take what the producers produce and distribute it, minus what it takes for itself. This is done by law, and the injustice keenly felt (even though we become adjusted to it), and thus we have friction. Remove the laws by which the producer is deprived of his product and order will prevail.

However, this speculation on the course of events if the individual should assume the duty of looking after public affairs, rather than leaving it to an elected official, is idle, or, to use a more modern term impregnated with sarcasm, "unrealistic." Not only would the politicians undertake to counteract the revolutionary non-voting movement, but many of the citizenry having a vested interest in the proceeds of taxation would raise a hue and cry about the "duty" of the citizen to vote. The teachers in our tax-supported schools would lecture their pupils on the lack of public spirit on the part of their parents. Propaganda would emanate from tax-exempt eleemosynary foundations, and from large manufacturers dependent on government contracts. Farmers' organizations, with an eye to government largess, veterans' societies asking for handouts, and particularly the bureaucracy, would denounce non-voting as a crime against society. In fact, all the "respectables" would join in proclaiming the movement revolutionary—which indeed it would be. It would be a revolution intended to shift the incidence of power from officialdom to the people.

We would be told, most emphatically, that by not voting we would be turning the reins of government over to "rascals." Probably so; but do we not regularly vote "rascals" out? And, after we have ousted one set, are we not called upon to oust another crew at the next election? It seems that rascality is endemic in government. Our balloting system has been defined as a battle of opposing forces, each armed with proposals for the public good, for a grant of power. As far as it goes, this definition is correct. But when the successful contestant acquires the grant of power toward what end does he use it—not theoretically but practically? Does he not, with an eye to the next election, go in for purchasing support, with the taxpayers' money, so that he might enjoy another period of power? The over-the-barrel method of seizing and maintaining political power is standard practice, and such is the nature of the "rascality."

This is not, however, an indictment of our election system. It is rather a rejection of the institution of the State. Our election system is merely one way of adjusting ourselves to that institution. The State is a product of conquest. As far back as we have any knowledge of the beginnings of this institution, it originated when a band of freebooting nomads swooped down on some peaceful group of agriculturists and picked up a number of slaves; slavery is the first form of economic exploitation. Repeated visitations of this sort left the victims breathless, if not lifeless and propertyless to boot. So, as people do when they have no other choice, they made a compromise with necessity; the peaceful communities hired one set of marauders to protect them from other thieving bands, for a price. In time, this tribute was regularized and was called taxation. The tax-gatherers settled down in the conquered communities, and though at first they were a people apart, time merged the two peoples—the conquerors and the conquered—into a nation. But, the system of taxation remained in force after it had lost its original character of tribute; lawyers and professors of economics, by deft circumlocution, turned tribute into "fiscal policy" and clothed it with social significance. Nevertheless, the effect of this system is to divide the citizenry into two classes: payers and receivers. Among those who live without producing are those who are called "servants of the people" and as such receive popular support. These further entrench themselves in their sinecures by setting up subtax-collecting allies who acquire a vested interest in the system; they grant these allies all sorts of privileges, such as franchises, tariffs, patents, subsidies and other something-for-nothing "rights." This division of spoils between those who wield power and those whose economic advantages depend on it is succinctly described as "the State within the State."

Thus, when we trace our political system to its origins we come to conquest. Tradition, law and custom have obscured its true nature, but no metamorphosis has taken place; its claws and fangs are still sharp, its appetite as voracious as ever. Politics is the art of seizing power for economic purposes. There is no doubt that men of character will give of talents for what they conceive to be the common good, without regard to their personal welfare. But, so long as our system of taxation is in vogue, so long as the political means of acquiring economic goods is available, just so long will the spirit of conquest assert itself; for men always seek to satisfy their desires with the least effort. It is interesting to speculate on the kind of campaigns and the type of candidates we would have if taxation were abolished and if, as a consequence, the power to dispense privileges was abolished. Who would run for office if "there were nothing in it?"

Why should any self-respecting citizen endorse an institution grounded on thievery? For that is what one does when one votes. If it be argued that we must let bygones be bygones, see what can be done toward cleaning up the institution of the State so that it might be useful in the maintenance of orderly existence, the answer is that it cannot be done; you cannot clean up a brothel and yet leave the business intact. We have been voting for one "good government" after another, and what have we got?

To effectuate the suggested revolution all that is necessary is for citizens to stay away from the polls. Unlike other revolutions, this one calls for no organization, no violence, no war fund, no leader to sell it out. In the quiet of his conscience each citizen pledges himself, to himself, not to give support to an immoral institution, and on election day stays home, or goes fishing. That's all. I started my revolution fifty years ago and the country is none the worse for it. Neither am I.

7

Abstain from Beans

by Robert LeFevre

John Roscoe and Ned Roscoe, Bagatorials *(New York: A Fireside Book published by Simon & Schuster, 1996), p. 17. Robert LeFevre (1911–1986) was a prolific libertarian author and founder of Freedom School/Rampart College.*

In ancient Athens, those who admired the Stoic philosophy of individualism took as their motto: "Abstain from Beans." The phrase had a precise reference. It meant: DON'T VOTE. To vote in Athens one dropped various-colored beans into a receptacle.

To vote is to express a preference. There is nothing implicitly evil in choosing. All of us in the ordinary course of our daily lives vote for or against dozens of products and services. When we vote for (buy) any good or service, it follows that by salutary neglect we vote against the goods or services we do not choose to buy. The great merit of marketplace choosing is that no one is bound by any other person's selection. I may choose Brand X. But this cannot prevent you from buying Brand Y.

When we place voting into the framework of politics, however, a major change occurs. When we express a preference politically, we do so precisely because we intend to bind others to our will. Political voting is the legal method we have adopted and extolled for obtaining monopolies of power. Political voting is nothing more than the assumption that might makes right. There is a presumption that any decision wanted by the majority of those expressing a preference must be desirable, and the inference even goes so far as to presume that anyone who differs from a majority view is wrong or possibly immoral.

But history shows repeatedly the madness of crowds and the irrationality of majorities. The only conceivable merit relating to majority rule lies in the fact that if we obtain monopoly decisions by this process, we will coerce fewer persons than if we permit the minority to coerce the majority. But implicit in all political voting is the necessity to coerce some so that all are controlled. The direction taken by the control is academic. Control as a monopoly in the hands of the state is basic.

In times such as these, it is incumbent upon free men and women to reexamine their most cherished, long-established beliefs. There is only one truly moral position for an honest person to take. He must refrain from coercing his fellows. This means that he should refuse to participate in the process by means of which some men obtain power over others. If you value your right to life, liberty, and property, then clearly there is every reason to refrain from participating in a process that is calculated to remove the life, liberty, or property from any other person. Voting is the method for obtaining legal power to coerce others.

8

The Illegality, Immorality, and Violence of All Political Action

by Robert LeFevre

LeFevre's Journal *(Vol. 1, No. 3, Summer 1974, pp. 1–3).*

There are only three arguments possible by which to try to justify the concept that some men may rightfully rule over other men and other men's property. Probably the earliest, and the most frequently employed, relates to force.

If I am big and strong enough, I may be able to rule you. Whether the force is obtained by superior military might, or by the presumed might of the most numerous group of voters expressed at the polls, the argument is the same. I'm big enough to have my will over you in any case; hence, my rule of you is just and proper.

The second to emerge is the appeal to a theological justification. God wills it; therefore, I have divine rights and may rightfully rule over you. I am special, set apart by the Almighty. Hence, I may rightfully seek to control you and your property, even if I should happen to lack the military force to do so.

The only other argument possible is the contractual one. You have voluntarily, as your own free act and deed, entered into an understanding with me in which you grant me certain decision-making functions over you and your property.

However, if we wish to be precise at this point, a contractual rule is not rule in any logical or legal sense. The separate contracting parties are always in a position to abrogate the contract and to renegotiate, whereas this is never true with government as we presently know it. The contractual argument is the gist of the Declaration of Independence.

The plight of the people of the United States is best summed up by recognizing that it is popularly believed that all three arguments are quite properly employed in our case.

It is presumed that (1) our government is strong enough to rule, therefore it may properly do so. (2) The Constitution is a divine instrument, the explicit result of heavenly supervision over the revolutionary leadership which brought about our separation from England, and thus, as a curious extension of that argument, while God has dethroned the king, God supervises elections and the voice of the people is the voice of God. (Vox populi, vox dei.) Further, (3) the creation of the governmental structure was contractual in nature, hence everything the government does is the result of a social contract to which we have all implicitly or explicitly agreed.

There is only one of these arguments that has any substance. The government is very strong and thus, because of its power, it may very well manage to rule. However, any pretense that the government has been divinely ordained or that some kind of social contract, explicit or implicit, exists between the government and those governed is pure nonsense.

Let me deal with the theological implications first. The very core of the resistance which led to the formation of this country as a separate nation, inspired by such men as Sam and John Adams, Jefferson, Hancock, Henry, Franklin, and a hundred others, rested its case on a denial of divine rights reposing in any man or body of men. It was the argument of those who signed the Declaration of Independence, or the Virginia Bill of Rights, and of Tom Paine in "Common Sense," that divine rights which raised some above others didn't and couldn't exist.

On the contrary, the position was taken that all men had precisely the same rights, no one having, or being able to obtain, any moral ascendancy over any other.

It is important to note that the documents referred to, which represented the axiomatic base to be established, clearly showed that all men's rights are *inalienable*. That can only mean that rights cannot be alienated. What these men were seeking to establish was the validity of a contractual government and the invalidity of any other kind of government. By no possible process whatever could any man obtain a right to rule any other—either by force of arms, by the voting process, or by other practices.

The denial of divine rights reposing in anyone, or obtainable by anyone, became the most dominant characteristic making up the belief of an American. Any pretense to divine rights was, hence, un-American, archaic, and relegated to the ash heap. It is on this point alone that we fought and obtained our independence.

Unfortunately, thirteen years after the signing of the Declaration, the entire concept of a contractual government was put aside. Instead, a single political party put together a governmental structure embodied in the Constitution which was not and never has been a social contract, and which has never been a statement coming from "we, the people of the United States."

Beginning approximately in 1785, a couple of years after the signing of the Treaty of Paris which brought about our legal severance from England, a political party calling itself the "Federalists" was organized. This small but determined group put together the so-called Constitutional Convention of 1787 and managed to obtain a majority approval of the instrument they had designed as a new form of government. The delegates were bound to return their findings to the state legislatures which had authorized their sojourn in Philadelphia for the convention. But this was never done. The Federalists well knew that the instrument they had framed would be disapproved by every state legislature then in existence. Hence they wrote into the Constitution, Article VII, the process of ratification, specifying that the Constitution would obtain ratification from the *conventions* of nine states. This made it possible for the Federalists to avoid virtually certain rejection by the state legislatures and also placed control of the conventions in their hands. As the only organized political party, they carefully packed the separate conventions, making certain not to convene any of them until they were reasonably certain of a successful vote. This procedure, by itself, wipes out any possible assumption of legality or moral obligation.

The Constitution was drawn up by a single political faction, was subsequently read by fewer than 10,000 (that is a generous estimate—it probably fell far short of that number), and was approved by simple majorities with a total of fewer than 6,000 delegates participating in scattered conventions. Opposition was strong and the Constitution barely squeaked by in some states. Thus, the instrument was drafted and approved, in the main, only by a few people within a single political party. Yet the instrument purports to come from "we, the people of the United States."

In view of the undeveloped communications system, the absence of roads, and the huge size of the rural populations, it is probable that a vast majority of Americans of European, Asian, or African origins didn't even know that conventions had been held or that an instrument had emerged claiming to be a contract with them.

At the time this was occurring, the total imported population was approximately three million people. By no stretch of the imagination can the deliberations of some six or seven thousand of that number be presumed to bind the total number within a contractual agreement.

In further support of this argument, the evidence shows that popular voting for presidents, beginning with George Washington, was so meager that no effort was made to preserve the figures. Thus, for the first ten presidential elections the only figures available are those showing electoral votes. However, in 1824, when no candidate obtained a majority of electoral votes and the election was decided in the House of Representatives, for the first time the popular totals were retained. The four candidates running that year polled an aggregate of 352,062, while the population of the United States according to the census of 1820 had reached a total of 9,638,453. Only slightly more than three per cent of the total population was voting even at this late date. The winning candidate in 1824, John Quincy Adams, received 105,321 votes, slightly more than one percent of the population of 1820. It is reasonable to assume that popular voting prior to 1824 was considerably less. There is no way these facts can be construed as evidence of a contract with the people of the United States.

As a result of the constant barrage of propaganda to which we are subjected, both directly from government and through the governmentally dominated and supported public school system, we have been led to believe that the American government has some kind of divine right to impose its will on us and to take our money and property and lives if it chooses. And if the divinity of the election process is denied, then it is argued that the Constitution came into existence as a result of a contractual understanding in which well-meaning persons entered into a voluntary association for mutual benefit. The facts are to the contrary.

Therefore, there is only one argument that can be validly applied to the American government. It rules because it has the power to rule. This is the justification of brute force. Every law, ukase, rule or bit of legislation enacted at federal, state, or local level is backed up by the ultimate threat of death. That may sound like an extreme statement, yet it is true, and applies even to traffic citations.

Let us suppose that a person has received a summons because he has allegedly violated some statute, law, or ruling. He decides that the summons is unjust and that he will not obey. The men in government decide that they will compel him to obey.

Clearly, it is always possible for men in or out of government to change their minds. The government can fail to prosecute, and a man who decides he will not submit to prosecution may ultimately decide to do so. But let us assume that both sides remain adamant.

What ensues? Legal formalities will be followed, of course. The unwilling target of the prosecution will receive a series of warnings, each more harsh than the last. Finally, since he will not obey, he will be physically arrested. But if he submits to arrest, he is in fact obeying. Therefore, he must resist arrest or confinement. Ultimately, he will be shot for resisting arrest or for trying to escape. The shot may not be fatal. But unless the man submits, he must keep trying to escape. In the end, death will be inflicted.

The ultimate truth is that even a traffic citation is backed up by an appeal to ultimate force to the point where death makes obedience impossible.

To assume that the people of the United States entered voluntarily into a contractual relationship of such unbalanced character that specific performance on the part of one of the contracting parties is enforced under the threat of death while specific performance on the part of the other contracting party is totally unenforceable, is a patent absurdity. No sane or reasonable human being would voluntarily bind himself by any such contract.

There is no way in which a remedy can be found for government that exists only by force, until the people at large understand that that is the only kind of government they have. However, this most assuredly does not imply, nor should it be inferred, that a government of force should be overturned by force. In my judgment, such should never be attempted. A forceful government forcefully eliminated, leaves forceful persons in control. The result is not a cure, but a further extension of the disease. There are available far more efficacious methods than an appeal to arms. The first and most important of these is an appeal to reason and to peace.

We have long been aware that slaves can be the product of monarchs and dictators. It is time we realized that slaves can also be produced by legislatures, and by executive decrees.

9

Where the Individual
Vote Really Counts

by Sy Leon

None of the Above: Why Non-Voters Are America's Political Majority *(San Fran-cisco: Fox & Wilkes, 1996), pp. 48–56. This excerpt comes from Chapter 6, and the book was originally published in 1976. Sy Leon refers to himself as an "anti-politician."*

It is fashionable these days to criticize governmental agencies and regulations. Even those who believe in the ability of government to solve our problems take swipes at the incredible bureaucratic waste and mis-management that occurs whenever a government "business" or regulatory agency decides to set up shop. Some politicians go so far as to support a "sunset" provision whereby agencies would have to justify their existence, say, every four years, or pass into oblivion.

Politicians, here and elsewhere, are taking a stand which they believe to be popular with the voters. We have become increasingly aware that business regulations, such as we find in various industries, which are sup-posed to "protect" the consumer from sundry evils, actually serve only to protect established firms from competing with other, more efficient or less costly businesses. Thus the consumer ends up paying more, not only for the service in question, but also for the support of the regulatory agen-cies themselves.

The same is true of government "services" in general. Anyone who has stood in line for what seems an eternity at a Department of Motor Vehicles or a post office, knows just how efficient these services are. And anyone who has tangled with an irate bureaucratic clerk, who need not worry about competition, knows just how courteous they can be.

With these everyday annoyances common to everyone, politicians invariably strike a responsive chord whenever they promise, as part of their campaign platforms, to minimize bureaucratic waste and inefficiency. The politicians, we are told, will clean up the bureaucracy if only we will vote for them. It is through the power of the vote, then, that we are supposed to express our wishes in regard to government agencies and services.

This is basically a sound idea. We should be able to make our desires known through a vote. But what the politicians fail to recognize is that we don't need them in order to do this. On the contrary, we cast dozens of votes every day without so much as one politician crossing our path. And this non-political voting system is so direct and efficient that the political method of voting is pale by comparison.

This remarkable voting system is economic, and the ballot is the dollar. Each time we buy something, we cast a vote in support of the company providing that product or service, thereby enabling it to stay in business. If we do not like a product, we do not buy it, thus casting a "no" vote. If we do like the product, we buy it, thus casting a "yes" vote. And if we don't like any brand of a particular item, we don't have to buy anything, thereby abstaining from the vote altogether.

With the economic vote there is no need for "sunset" provisions. A business operating on the principles of a voluntary market will succeed only as long as its customers remain satisfied. A shoe manufacturer need not prove its usefulness to a band of politicians. Its usefulness is reinforced every day, as consumers continue to buy its product. If and when consumers withhold their economic vote, the business will quickly disappear.

If those who support and advocate the political system of voting are as enamored as they claim to be about the sanctity of the vote, and if they want voting to express the will of the people, then consistency demands that they champion the economic vote above the political vote. They should institute steps to accelerate moving governmental services and agencies to the private sector, where consumers can voice their satisfaction or dissatisfaction directly by either supporting or not supporting those agencies. This, of course, would be a dangerous political move because politicians are well aware that the vast majority of government activities could not sustain themselves in a voluntary market. Indeed, this is especially true of the "services" provided by politicians themselves. If subjected to an economic vote, whereby we had a choice of whether to hire a politician or not, politicians would quickly find themselves in the unemployment line.

But, it may be asked, isn't this just crass materialism? Why should everything be reduced to the crude level of dollars and cents? It is, after all, quite possible that many government services are worthwhile even if they could not survive in the private sector.

In response to this, we should note that the economic vote is not just a matter of dollars and cents, any more than the political vote is just a matter of pulling a lever in a voting booth. True, we cast our economic votes through dollars and cents, just as we cast our political votes by pulling levers, but that money is simply the means by which we make our desires known. The economic vote is important because it represents free choice. Each time we make a purchase, by casting an economic vote, we express a preference and make our desires known. This is the means by which we control our own destiny and determine the course of our lives. And, in the final analysis, isn't this what self-rule is supposed to be about?

There is an argument in favor of political voting to the effect that although voting for politicians to represent us and make our decisions is not desirable, voting on the issues themselves—in the form of propositions—is a direct way of expressing our choices. It eliminates the political "middlemen" and lets the individual voter choose, for instance, whether or not tax revenue should be used for education, whether or not the use of nuclear energy should be forbidden, and so on. It's a good argument, too, as far as it goes. It just doesn't go far enough. Again, when we vote on the various propositions, we decide the issues not just for ourselves but for others. If the majority of voters are opposed to something, they are making a choice for the rest, who favor it. It is only in the economic marketplace that the *individual* vote really counts.

Most of us are aware of the pitfalls of committee action. The larger the committee, the more confusing and unsatisfactory the results of its decisions. And the largest, most inefficient committee of all is the voting public. History shows that most progress has occurred in spite of public opinion, not because of it.

If the introduction of electricity, supermarkets, airplanes, and an endless list of inventions that improved the quality of life, had been put to a vote, we'd be without them today. Only because an individual got an idea and *was free* to risk his own time and money to implement it, has a wider range of choices been made available to the public. And when the public, on an individual basis, rejected the product offered by an individual, only he had to bear the cost involved.

If the decision to produce Volkswagens and Rolls-Royces had been put to a vote, most people would have rejected them: The former would have been too ugly and too cheap for other cars to compete with it; the latter too unnecessarily luxurious. But it wasn't up to the public *en masse*, only as individuals—and as individuals the public "voted" in their favor. The consequence of this individual, *economic* vote is a wider range of choice, an increased number of jobs and a greater wealth circulating in the economy. If the public had cast its economic votes against them (as it did with the Edsel), they would have been removed from the market and only the individual businessmen promoting them would have suffered.

Why is the economic vote superior to the political vote? First, we are able to buy a finished product; we are not voting merely for a promise to do something, which is all we ever get from politicians. When we buy a service, we have a contractual guarantee that the service will be performed satisfactorily, which is something no politician dares to do.

Second, we have true choice with our economic vote. We can abstain from voting altogether by refusing to buy any brand of a particular item. No product or service can be forced upon us. If we dislike or disagree with what is being offered, we are not forced to pay for it or use it. This, unfortunately, is the opposite of what occurs in politics.

Third, we vote only for ourselves, not for other people. Through the economic vote we express our personal preferences, but we do not make decisions for other people. They are as free as we are to choose for themselves.

Fourth, we can vote every day, and we can continually revise our vote in the face of new information. If we decide from one day to the next that we do not like a product, or that we like another product better, we can put our decision into effect immediately. This is not the case, however, with the political vote. We can cast our political vote only once every several years, and we are stuck with the decision in the meantime.

Fifth, we can vote for particulars with our economic vote. We can cast one vote for the kind of detergent we want, another vote for the kind of television set we want, and so fourth. This allows us to retain complete control over our lives. When we elect a political candidate on the other hand, he presumes to make specific choices for us. We do not have that fine-tuning control with which the economic vote provides us.

Finally, through the economic vote we are able to express our desires directly, without using an intermediary. With the political vote, however, another person claims to act in our behalf, and we are forced to pay for his services through money stolen by taxation.

These are only a few of the advantages of the economic vote. But even if the politician agrees that the economic vote is superior to the political vote in many respects, he may offer the final defense that we need some of each. The economic vote and the political vote, he may argue, should exist side by side.

The problem with this suggestion is that it is impossible. The economic and political vote are not only different, they are incompatible. The key to the economic vote is the voluntary consent and cooperation of all participants. The aim of economic voting is to satisfy all parties concerned through a process of mutual exchange. Herein lies the power of economic voting to satisfy individual desires, and herein lies its basic antagonism to the political process.

As is made clear in other chapters of this book, political voting is a process whereby one group of people attempts to force its desires on the rest of the people in a country. The more areas of our lives that are determined by political voting, the less individual choice we have. This is, after all, the problem with governmental agencies, which are the consequence of political rather than economic voting, with the result that they are totally insensitive to consumer desires and demands. We are prevented from exercising our economic vote with these agencies for the simple reason that free choice has been pushed aside by political decree.

In advocating a voters' boycott we are referring to the political vote. We oppose voting not because we want people to have less say in their own affairs but because we want them to have more say. In other words, the less political voting we have, the more economic voting will be possible. And the more we are able to vote economically, the more choice we have. Opposition to the political vote, therefore, is really a positive program aimed at enriching each of our lives.

10

Is Voting a Moral Act?

by Robert Ringer

Restoring the American Dream *(New York: QED, 1979), pp. 285–287. This excerpt is taken from Chapter 9, "Taking Back America." Robert Ringer is a well known writer and author of* Looking Out for #1.

There is a very serious question as to the morality of the act of voting.

It certainly is not moral to commit aggression against others; yet when you vote for a candidate, you are voting to put someone in a position to rule the lives of your fellowmen—men who either do not want that candidate to rule them or do not want *anyone* to rule them. And if it is an issue you are voting for or against, you are usually voting to interfere with the lives of those who are on the opposite side of such an issue.

Another moral consideration is whether you are voting for someone because you genuinely favor his governing you or because you are adhering to the time-honored approach of most voters—voting for the "lesser of two evils."

Suppose that Candidate A, by your standards, is unfit for public office; likewise, you feel that Candidate B is unqualified to represent you. Is it still your patriotic duty to vote for one of these two men? Should you obediently cast your vote for the "lesser of two evils"—an election ritual that has been performed by untold millions—and cast your vote for *someone*?

As Sy Leon has explained, those who adhere to this philosophy ignore one important moral reality: *The lesser of two evils is still evil!*

Every time you vote for someone whom you consider to be the lesser of two evils, you cast a vote not for someone whom you genuinely desire to have represent you, but for despair. It is an admission on your part that you cannot fight The System—which may be true, but that does not mean you must contribute to its perpetuation.

The person who votes for a candidate simply because he is not as bad as the other candidate is the one who is apathetic; he is symbolically throwing in the towel via his ballot. He is, in effect, encouraging a politician whom he considers to be evil to believe that he represents "the people."

Those who persist in clinging to the old cliché about "not being able to change the system unless you participate" are missing the whole point: it doesn't matter who wins! History has proven that participation has absolutely nothing whatsoever to do with change....

... We have come a long way since men first believed that the sun revolved around the earth. Now it is time that we grew up and faced the reality that government does not represent us. Candidates are elected by an elite group of men and women who have managed to finesse their way through the political maze that leads to the inner circle of the establishment. The lesser-of-two-evils voting philosophy merely validates the right of government to perpetuate this ruse.

In view of the realities of The System, does a nonvoter really "get what he deserves?" Hardly. Since he has, in effect, voted in favor of not being ruled, what he really deserves is to be left alone. Nonetheless, politicians maintain that if you do not vote, you have no right to complain. They tell you that you are apathetic. That is like telling a man he is apathetic if he refuses to choose between having either his TV set or his watch stolen. It is absurd to conclude that because such a man refuses to "vote" on which crime should be committed against him, he "deserves it" when one of the two items is stolen. If the ballot does not provide you with a choice to your liking, how else can you exercise your so-called freedom of choice except by not voting?

You have a natural right to say no to anything. And when you decline to vote, you are saying no to *all* the candidates. When someone chastises you for not voting, isn't he really saying that you have no *right* to exercise a "no" vote?

The truth is that the person who refuses to vote (for moral and/or intellectual reasons) shows far more love of his country, and far more courage, than the lesser-of-two-evils robot. Instead of simply falling into line, such a dissenter is, in effect, saying, "I refuse to go along with illogical rhetoric; I refuse to be intimidated by patriotic slogans; I refuse to be coerced by promises of 'getting what I deserve' should I not exercise my 'right' to vote; I refuse to be deceived into believing that I have a free choice."

The average citizen, intent on doing the moral thing, does not realize that there is an alternative open to him aside from voting for one of two candidates of whom he disapproves. He can cast a vote of dissent, thus communicating to government that he opposes *both* candidates and does not wish to have either one represent him.

Massive nonvoting could conceivably put an end, once and for all, to the dangerous illusion that "the people have chosen." If nonvoters (the *real* silent majority) gained enough support, it is conceivable that politicians might adopt libertarian reforms to appease such a massive nonvoting majority.

To say the least, it certainly would be difficult for a winning candidate who received 5% of the votes of eligible voters to claim to have a "mandate of the people." And it would be very unconvincing to try to accuse 80% or 90% of the population of being "apathetic."

Yet one must never forget the reality that politicians have no shame. With nonvoters already piling up an overwhelming majority of nearly two to one over the "winner" of each presidential election, politicians still refuse to acknowledge the discontent of the majority and simply pass off nonvoters as "apathetic."

Whether or not to vote is something you must decide for yourself. But you should consider all aspects very seriously, not only from an intellectual standpoint, but from the standpoints of morality and practicality.

11

Should Libertarians Vote or Hold Political Office?

by George Smith

"Party Dialogue" in Carl Watner, George H. Smith, & Wendy McElroy, Neither Bullets nor Ballots: Essays on Voluntaryism *(Orange: Pine Tree Press, 1983), pp. 9–28. This article first appeared in Sam Konkin's* New Libertarian *(Vol. IV, No. 8, Dec. 1980–Feb. 1981). George H. Smith is author of* Atheism: The Case Against God.

Libertarian Party Advocate *(LPer):* Considering the success that the Libertarian Party has enjoyed in recent years, especially in bringing libertarian ideas to the attention of the general public, I am curious why you refuse to support the LP—in fact, you criticize it openly.

Anti-Political Libertarian *(APL):* You raise two issues that need to be untangled. First, I criticize the *political* side of the LP, *i.e.,* its effort to place libertarians in political office. I don't object to its educational endeavors, as I don't object to any organization that seeks to roll back the State.

Secondly, it is true that the LP gains publicity, but we must ask whether this is the *kind* of publicity that furthers libertarian goals. Publicity that links libertarianism to a political party—when the essence of libertarianism is anti-political—is counterproductive.

LPer: But the public understands that the LP is a party with a difference; it is devoted to liberty. That is the important thing.

APL: You beg the question. Can a political party be dedicated to uncompromised liberty? I answer, "No," and this is why I reject the LP.

LPer: I disagree. There is no reason why libertarian legislators could not dedicate themselves to the repeal of unjust laws. We must remember that the ultimate goal of the LP is a free society.

APL: Let's separate campaign rhetoric from reality. It's easy to say that the goal of the LP is a free society. What political party in its right mind would come out *against* a "free" society. The important point is:

Should Libertarians Vote or Hold Political Office? (Smith)

51

What makes the LP a *political* party? What is its *essential* characteristic? In other words, what does the LP have in common with other political parties that it does not share with nonpolitical organizations? The answer is simple: the LP seeks *political power*. The immediate goal of the LP *qua* political party, is (and must be) to wrest control of the State apparatus from its competitors, the Democrats and Republicans. The LP bids in the political auction, using the currency of votes in an attempt to buy control of the State machinery.

LPer: You're really off-base. The LP does not seek power. On the contrary, it wants to reduce power by dismantling the State. Getting elected to political office is simply a *means* to this noble end.

APL: Let's be clear about this. There is a difference between having power and exercising it. Those who control the State have immense power, whether or not they exercise it in particular instances. Political power—the capacity and legal sanction to aggress against others—is integral to political office. A State official, libertarian or not, has considerable power over defenseless citizens. It is disingenuous to claim that one aspires to political office but does not seek power. Power is a defining characteristic of political office.

LPer: But this is mere semantics! A libertarian politician might have "power" in a legal sense, but he would not use that power unjustly. His power would be used to combat other politicians and to repeal invasive laws.

APL: You have just conceded my point. Legal power, which you dismiss so lightly, is what makes a politician a politician. A politician can get together with his neighbors (other politicians) and vote to rob people, and he can bring the force of law to back up this vote. But if I and my neighbors vote to rob someone, we cannot do it with the sanction of law. The politician has this political power, whereas the private citizen does not. This characteristic of political office must never be forgotten.

You admit that even the libertarian politician will have this power after he is elected, but you stipulate that it will be used for beneficent purposes. You prefer to emphasize the (presumed) *motives* of libertarian politicians—their honorable intentions; whereas I prefer to stress the *reality* of what political office entails. I don't want *anyone* to have political power, regardless of his supposed good intentions. I object to the political office itself and to its legitimized power. Frankly, I don't give a whit about the psychological state of the politician.

LPer: You seem to be saying that you don't trust the libertarian politician to keep his word. Well, we live in an imperfect world with no absolute guarantees. We hope that libertarian politicians will not compromise. If they do, we shall be the first to denounce them.

APL: The issue of trust is quite secondary. Whether I trust this or that politician is not the point, although it does raise an interesting problem. Should the wise maxim often quoted by libertarians, "Power corrupts," now be amended to read, "Power corrupts—unless you are a libertarian?" It is not clear to me why libertarians are any less susceptible to the temptations of power than the ordinary mortal.

But, as I said, this is not fundamental. I may trust a particular libertarian politician, but I still don't want him to have political power over me. Libertarians stress that liberty is a natural right. If a legal/political system violates this right as a matter of policy, then the system is unjust to some degree. Libertarians should oppose this injustice *in principle*. We should seek to abolish the mechanism whereby one individual, in virtue of political office, can employ legitimized aggression against other individuals.

"Elect me to office," proclaims the libertarian politician, "give me enormous power over you and your property, but rest assured that I shall abstain from using this power unjustly." I reply: You have no right to such power in the first place—and as a libertarian you should know this. You should be *denouncing* the very office to which you aspire. You say your campaign literature is honest and forthright, Mr. would-be-Senator; but search as I may I cannot find the statement, "The office of Senator, as we know it, should be abolished." This lacuna is understandable, however, in view of the embarrassment that the statement would cause you. For then even a child might be prompted to ask: "But Mr. would-be-Senator, if the institution of senator is wrong in itself (because of its built-in political power), then how can you, in good conscience, ask us to make you a Senator?"

LPer: You bog down in technicalities. This business about the incompatibility of libertarianism and political office is just so much theoretical fluff. Let's get down to the real world. I still don't see why a libertarian Senator could not consistently and conscientiously work for the elimination of unjust laws.

APL: If you don't see it, it is because (to paraphrase Plato) you have eyes but no intelligence. You don't see the answer because you don't ask the right question. We don't start with the concept of a "Libertarian Senator" and then inquire whether this person can be trusted. The basic difficulty is with the concept of a "Libertarian Senator" to begin with.

"Libertarian" and "Senator" (for Senator, read: "any political office")

Should Libertarians Vote or Hold Political Office? (Smith)

53

are like a square and a circle. One cannot be both at the same time and in the same respect. The "technicality" to which you object is the law of noncontradiction.

What does it mean, in this society, to be a Senator? Among other things, it signifies the legal privilege to formulate and enact laws without any necessary regard for the justice of those laws, and it permits one to dispense massive amounts of stolen money. Such powers, inherent in the office of Senator, are incompatible with libertarian principles. *Libertarians should oppose not just this or that Senator, but the office of "Senator" itself.*

LPer: But couldn't a libertarian accept a political office while being fully aware that the legal power inherent in that office is illegitimate? He need not exercise the options legally available to him, after all. As a libertarian, he would know that he has no right to act unjustly, regardless of his political situation.

APL: You confuse the subjective with the objective. A person can believe just about anything. A libertarian Senator may believe that he is faking it, that he doesn't really take the authority of his office seriously. He may convince himself that, although an agent and employee of the State, he is really and truly anti-state. It is similarly possible, I suppose, for an army general to convince himself that he is anti-military despite his occupation. Whether this kind of subversion from within is good strategy is a topic for another conversation. But the facts remain. The office of Senator is defined independently of the desires of individual Senators. The powers of political office do not depend upon the secret desires of the LP politician, nor do they change because the politician keeps his fingers crossed while taking the oath of office.

One cannot deny the legitimacy of the Senatorial office, as libertarians must logically do, and simultaneously advocate someone for that position. One should not accept the designation of "Senator," knowing full-well what this implies, while mouthing libertarian principles.

Consider an extreme case. If we lived under a dictatorship, would the LP advocate that a libertarian take over the office of dictator, or would it fight for the abolition of dictatorship itself?

LPer: Abolition must certainly be the goal of any libertarian. This doesn't mean, however, that abolition could not be achieved through the former method. It would be preferable to have a libertarian "dictator" who refuses to exercise the powers of his office, rather than an authentic dictator. Don't you agree?

APL: If we must have a dictator, then I prefer to have the most benign one possible. But a benign dictator is still a dictator; and if there were a group of self-professed "libertarians" who were expending their time, energy, and resources in an effort to put their version of a benign dictator in power to replace the current one, then I would have grave doubts about their libertarian credentials. And I would view their candidate for dictator as a threat, even if one less serious than the present dictator.

LPer: So you would support the libertarian "dictator."

APL: No. I would not support *any* dictator. I might prefer your dictator to the current one, but I wouldn't support either of them. If I am given a choice between Mr. Jones, who plans to cut off my head, and Mr. White, who plans to cut off my hands, then I may *prefer* Mr. White to Mr. Jones, since I would rather lose my hands than my head. But I certainly wouldn't support or condone either Mr. Jones or Mr. White. Both are my enemies, even if one is relatively less harmful than the other.

We must not forget the central point. Your dictator might be preferable to another dictator. There are obvious differences in degree. But we are concerned not only with the relative demerits of dictators, but with the possibility that one can be a dictator and a libertarian at the same time. Can libertarians actively support and promote a benign dictator, just because he might be the best dictator available? This is a peculiar situation indeed, and it would force libertarians to support the lesser of two evils.

In short, I would not call your candidate for dictator a libertarian, because the two are incompatible. I might call him a well-intentioned dictator, but he is no libertarian. And I would oppose him, because my principles leave me no option. There is no proviso in my stand against dictators that exempts those with good intentions.

Similarly, your Libertarian Senator may do less harm (and even some positive good) when compared to Democrats and Republicans. He may reduce taxes, for example, or help avoid war. But fewer taxes and peace are not distinctively libertarian positions; some conservatives and liberals advocate the same things. What distinguishes libertarianism is the *basis* for its opposition to taxes and war (the rights of the individual) and the logical extreme to which it carries its opposition. Most importantly, there is the libertarian analysis of the State as a ruling elite—the fundamental cause of taxes and war. The oppressive nature of the State is at the core of libertarian theory, and it requires libertarians to take a principled stand against the State *per se.* Now the State is an institution with different levels of authority, and it is this authority—legitimized aggression, as I described earlier—which libertarians must oppose.

You see, therefore, that libertarians must stand firm against *all*

Should Libertarians Vote or Hold Political Office? (Smith)

55

Senators, *all* Presidents, and so forth, because these offices and the legal power they embody are indispensable features of the State apparatus. After all, *what can it possibly mean to oppose the State unless one opposes particular offices and institutions in which State power manifests itself?* Do we dislike President Carter because he has the wrong ideas? No. We dislike him because he is dangerous, and *he is dangerous because he is President.* Millions of individuals may have even worse ideas than Carter, but we don't single them out for disdain unless they are in a position to *enforce* their views. The danger lies not in Carter but in the Presidency. Carter derives his power from the office and its legal sanction. The political office itself is the fundamental danger, and that is what we must strive to eliminate. Certainly Carter is a dangerous man, but anyone who is President is dangerous as well. The Presidency embodies political power on an enormous scale, and any person occupying that office, "libertarian" or not, must be opposed by right-thinking libertarians.

LPer: Well, your ultimate goals are commendable, but you live in a fantasy world. You don't really believe that political offices are just going to fade away, do you?

APL: No, but neither do I believe that a group of libertarians are going to take over the government, establish themselves in power, and then attempt to abolish the instrument of their power and livelihood, the State. Now there is a real fantasy.

LPer: So what do you suggest instead? It's one thing to criticize, but its more difficult to map an alternate strategy.

APL: First of all, let's get something straight. This is *not*—I repeat, *not*—an issue of strategy. You LPers seem to have difficulty in understanding this, so I have to place special emphasis on it. I am not accusing the LP of faulty strategy here (although this is a lively topic for another discussion). This is not simply a matter of how to get from here to there.

LPer: But we both agree on the desirability of a free society. It seems to me that we just disagree on how best to achieve it.

APL: Yes, we are in basic agreement concerning the goal to be achieved. But I am not merely asserting that the political method is *inefficient* in pursuit of this goal. Rather, I am arguing that the political means is *inconsistent* with libertarian principles, that it flies in the face of basic libertarian ideals. Consider an analogy. I state that a basic goal in my life is to acquire a good deal of money. You concede that this goal is, in itself, unobjectionable. Then I proceed to rob a bank. You are horrified and demand to know how I could do such a thing. I reply that we have a strategic difference of opinion. We both agree that my goal is laudable;

we simply disagree concerning the means by which to attain it. We disagree on how to get from here to there. So I demand from you an alternative strategy for me to get rich. Sure, I say, my plan may not be perfect, but what can you purists offer in it place? Give me an alternate strategy, I demand, before taking pot shots at mine.

How would you reply to this? I suspect that you would accuse me of shifting ground. You would point out that the objection to robbing banks is not a simple issue of strategy, but involves profound moral questions. And you would say that your protest against my action was moral, rather than strategic, in nature. Therefore, unless I can surmount the moral objections to robbing banks, the strategy question is irrelevant. I cannot squirm past the moral issues, the matters of principle, in the guise of demanding alternate strategies.

Now, returning to the subject of political action, I respond to your question the same way. Fine, let's get together and talk over the issue of strategy some day—we can talk about education, moral suasion, counter-economics, alternative institutions, civil disobedience, or what have you—but that's not the issue here. I submit that there is a profoundly anti-libertarian aspect of political action—*i.e.,* of attempting to elect libertarians to public office—and this is the issue to which political libertarians must first address themselves. Show me that political action is consistent with libertarian principles, and then we can take up the issue of strategy.

LPer: But you must address yourself to the issue of strategy at some point. You wish to disqualify the political means altogether, which seems to leave you precious little by which you can work for a free society. If your principles condemn you to inaction and certain defeat, then surely there must be something wrong with your principles.

APL: This is quite curious. You equate activism with political action. Doing something, for you means, doing something political. You regard an anti-political libertarian as a non-activist, and this is surely one of the most pernicious myths circulating in the LP today. Often, when LP members learn that I am not a member of the "The Party," I am greeted with the cute remark: "Oh, you're a libertarian with a small '1.'" To this I frankly feel like replying, "Yes, and you're an Idiot with a big 'I.'"

LPer: O.K., so you don't advocate inaction or passivity. Then what kind of activity, in your view, should libertarians engage in?

APL: I will state what I regard as the major challenge confronting libertarians today, and from this you could justify any number of different strategies. Here is the basic issue.

The fight against the State is not merely a fight against naked

Should Libertarians Vote or Hold Political Office? (Smith)

57

power—the battle would be much easier if that were so. The essence of the State is not aggression *per se,* but *legitimized* aggression. The State uses the sanction of law to legitimize its criminal acts. This is what distinguishes it from the average criminal in the street.

Unfortunately, the reality of the State—what it is in fact—is not how it is perceived by most Americans. To put it bluntly, the vast majority of Americans disagree with the libertarian view of the State. We may get some agreement on particular points, but the vision of the State as, in essence, a criminal gang, is far more radical than most Americans are willing to accept.

This defines our ultimate educational goal. We must strip the State of its legitimacy in the public eye. We must persuade people to apply the same moral standards to the State as they apply to anyone else. We need not convince people that theft is wrong; we need to convince them that theft, when committed by the State in the name of taxation, does not differ from theft when committed by an individual. We need not persuade people that murder is wrong; we need to persuade them that murder, when committed by the State in the name of war or national defense, does not differ from murder when committed by an individual.

As I said before, political power represents legitimized aggression. Libertarians may not be able to stop all aggression—this would indeed be an unrealistic goal—but they can go far in stripping political aggression of its moral sanctity. This requires all the tools of persuasion that we can muster, and it also underscores the illegitimacy of political action. To run for or support candidates for political office is to grant legitimacy to the very thing we are attempting to strip of legitimacy. One cannot consistently denounce the State as a band of criminals while attempting to swell the ranks of this criminal class with one's own cronies. The hypocrisy is there for all to see. So either you have to reject political action, or you have to waterdown or abandon your basic principles in order to conceal the glaring inconsistency. Some people call this latter alternative, being practical. I call it being dishonest and hypocritical.

LPer: So you don't think libertarians should run for political office. Does this mean that libertarians shouldn't vote either?

APL: Definitely, but there is more involved than simply not voting. Libertarians should *oppose* the vote in principle—they should oppose the mechanism by which political sanctification occurs. Political power is legitimized through the electoral process. The present voting system is based on the premise that fundamental rights can be gained or surrendered depending on the vote total. Libertarians must oppose this unconscionable process. We must oppose the political process itself—the mechanism whereby some persons gain unjust (but legitimized) power over others.

The vote sanctifies injustice. If the libertarian message is to be truly radical—if libertarians are to lead the fight, not only against this or that injustice, but against the political system that perpetuates and legitimizes injustice—then we must condemn voting altogether. A libertarian cannot use the vote for his own end, as if the vote were morally neutral. The vote is the method by which the State maintains its illusion of legitimacy. There is no way a libertarian organization can assail the legitimacy of the State while soliciting votes.

LPer: You make it sound as if pulling a lever in the election booth is an aggressive act. But it's not, and there's no way you can equate the two, particularly if one votes for a libertarian.

APL: Voting is not an aggressive act in the narrow sense. But politicians don't aggress in this sense either. A President or Senator doesn't personally go out and arrest or strong-arm people who disobey their decrees. It's possible that President Carter has never personally committed an aggressive act in his life. President Johnson didn't personally travel to Vietnam to murder Vietnamese. Does this mean that libertarians cannot regard these politicians as violators of human rights? Of course not. We are dealing with a chain of command where the upper echelon does not have to implement its own dirty work. Referring to my earlier point, however, President Johnson did not have the moral right to order the murder of innocent Vietnamese; and no politician has the moral right to order the violation of rights, however small.

Now let's apply this idea to the voting booth. To be elected to public office is to gain the legal sanction to aggress. This is a fact, whether we like it or not, and whether a given politician uses his power or not. But there is no corresponding *moral* right. The political right to aggress is a legal fiction without foundation in moral law.

I maintain, therefore, that no person has the *moral* right to vote. To vote a person into office is to give that person unjust authority over others. To vote for a presidential candidate is to grant to that person the legal sanction for injustice. Let us suppose that an LPer votes for Ed Clark for President. If Ed Clark were elected, he would, in his capacity as President, have the legal right of aggression. For instance, he could order the incarceration of political dissidents during a "national emergency." But there is no such moral right as this. It is the usurpation of rights. And just as Ed Clark does not have the moral right to this kind of power, so

Should Libertarians Vote or Hold Political Office? (Smith)

59

no one has the right to grant him that power, or to legitimize that power. When an LPer enters the voting booth, he is attempting to place in office a person who will have unjust authority over me. But, claims the LPer, his candidate will not use that power. I reply that this, even if true, is immaterial. The legitimized power embodied in the political office *is not his to give in the first place.* The LPer does not have the right to aggress against me, and it is sheer presumption to assume that he has the right to grant this privilege to his political favorite. How the libertarian, of all people, can calmly grant his political candidate the legal right to aggress without the slightest qualms—when all libertarians know that one cannot transfer rights that one does not have in the first place—escapes my understanding.

LPer: Again, I sympathize with your point of view, but I must bring you back to the real world. In an ideal libertarian society there would not exist voting as we know it—agreed. But in this world, voting is the method by which political change is effected, for better or worse. Today libertarians should vote as a matter of self-defense. The government aggresses against us and will continue to aggress unless we fight back, using its own weapons, if need be. Surely you wouldn't deny to libertarians the right to vote in self-defense, as a means of fighting against the encroachment of state power. One can use the vote in this way without lending it moral sanction.

APL: Again I am accused of not living in the real world. May I suggest that this jab applies more to you than to me. I have argued that we should take a good, hard look at the world of politics. What is the State? What is the nature of political office? You reply that this is immaterial? Why? Because libertarian candidates are brimming over with good intentions. They will sneak up on the State and turn this engine of monstrous power against itself. They will win the voting game, and all the bad politicians will gracefully concede defeat, pick up their marbles, and go home in pursuit of honest work.

Next I argued that voting entails empowering someone to act as your agent, and that you cannot morally grant to your agent rights which you do not properly possess. Moreover, I pointed out that the vote is the basis of political legitimacy in America today. It is the taproot of political authority in the minds of most Americans. Now this is a hard fact, whether we like it or not. You reply that this doesn't matter, that libertarians can overlook these inconvenient details. Other people, you argue, may think that we approve of voting and the political process because we run candidates for office, just like every political party, and because we encourage people to vote, just like every political party. Those poor silly people. They obviously don't realize that, despite appearances, we are really against voting and political power. Deep down inside we really oppose these things. It's just that we have to defend ourselves.

To your plea of self-defense, I reply: Fine, defend yourself, but leave me alone. But voting is wrong precisely because it does not leave me alone. If you elect your candidate to office in the name of self-defense, his power will not be restricted to you and to those who voted for him. He will have power over me and others like me as well.

When you enter the voting booth, you are committing an act of enormous presumption. You presume that you have the right to appoint a political guardian over me—a benevolent one, you claim, but a guardian nonetheless. Now as one libertarian to another, I must repeat my question: Where did you get such a right? You have no special authority over me. Where, then, did you obtain the right to appoint an agent with this authority? Where do you get the nerve to advocate that Ed Clark (or anyone else) should have the power of life and death over me and millions of other Americans? You claim self-defense. I claim that your vote extends far beyond the legitimate boundaries of self-defense.

LPer: You place great stress on this notion of abstract political power, which you say is the legal right to aggress, and you claim that the vote sanctions this power, whether or not a particular politician exercises it. It is primarily on this basis that you exclude political action. It seems to me that you sacrifice a strategy with great potential in the name of this abstract notion. We confront real-life crises, questions of economic survival and even of life-and-death. If we can elect politicians who will roll back the powers of the State, and who will not use those unjust powers inherent in their offices, then I say we contribute greatly to the cause of liberty.

APL: You miss the point of much of what I said. I, as an individual, do not somehow forbid political action. I contend that libertarian principles forbid it. You find this inconvenient, and you complain. I say, if you wish to complain, then complain about the principles, not about me. Political action conflicts with libertarian opposition to legitimized aggression—political power. Consistency demands, that I reject it. I accept libertarianism, and this very acceptance compels me to reject political action.

Therefore, when I am told that political action is a good strategy to achieve libertarian goals, I can only reply: Even if that were true (which I don't accept), it would not change the rightness involved. As the poet Heine once wrote: "We do not take possession of our ideas, but are possessed by them. They master us and force us into the arena, where, like

Should Libertarians Vote or Hold Political Office? (Smith)

61

gladiators, we must fight for them." So here I am, logically mastered by the consistency of libertarianism, forced into the arena to fight against political action.

LPer: You anti-party types amaze me. Here we have thousands of dedicated libertarians working to change things in America, and you purists sit in your ivory towers carping away. Words, words, words! If libertarians listened to you purists, nobody would do anything, and government power would continue to increase. I suppose you'll still be spouting your principles when the State comes to haul you off to jail.

APL: If the State hauls me off to jail then, yes, I will still be spouting my principles, especially if it's a libertarian State that does the hauling. You accuse me of purism. I reply, "So what?" If "purism" means anything, it means the refusal to budge on matters of principle even at the expense of apparent short-term gains. What is the alternative? "Impurism?" "Corruptism?" "Selling outism?"

And as long as we're discussing amazing things, let's go back to the issue of strategy of which you seem so fond. Hasn't it ever struck you as paradoxical how libertarians who are innovative when it comes to free-market alternatives, can be so pedestrian and orthodox in the area of political strategy. I mean, libertarians never tire of outlining plans for free-market roads, sewers, utilities, charities, schools, police forces, and even courts of law. When our critics ridicule free-market education, for instance, we encourage them to expand their thinking and to reject the notion that just because government has provided something in the past, it must continue to provide it in the future. Fresh, imaginative thinking is the key here. But now comes the issue of political strategy, and the imaginative libertarian suddenly turns slavishly orthodox. "How can we change things," he asks, "without political action? Nobody, especially the media, will pay any attention to us. Everyone knows that you have to muster the power of votes before you can change things significantly. We must get petitions signed; we must get our people on the ballot; we must get them elected to office—this is the only effective way to implement our goals."

To this political libertarian, I say: "If you spent a fraction of the time considering alternatives to political action as you do considering alternatives to public roads, utilities, etc., something might occur to you. You spend thousands of dollars and expend thousands of hours to get petitions signed and run political campaigns. If you spent a fraction of that energy and money on nonpolitical alternatives, you might witness a degree of progress that you now consider impossible.

LPer: But you're forgetting about the government and its repressive laws. Somebody, at some time, must work to repeal those laws. Education, counter-economics, civil disobedience, alternative institutions—all those things sound good, but of what use are they unless they result in the repeal of laws and regulations that restrict our freedom? And this repeal necessarily entails political action.

APL: First, it's not true that laws have to be repealed in order to be rendered ineffective. There are thousands of laws on the books today which are virtually dead, because the public would not tolerate their enforcement.

Second, there are always plenty of political hacks around who will attempt to curry favor by doing whatever is popular with the general public. Laws will become ineffective or will be repealed when it becomes impossible to enforce them—when the public sentiment overwhelmingly opposes them.

This brings me to a fundamental difference in our view of what libertarians should strive for. You wish to work directly through the political process. I maintain that this reinforces the legitimacy of that process. You tell people, in effect, that the way to assert their natural rights is to ask the government's permission. When the government gives you permission to keep your earnings, or to teach your children, or to live a particular lifestyle, then it's O.K. to do so. It's all very proper; the game is played by the State's own rules.

I maintain on the contrary, that libertarians should breed a thorough and uncompromising disrespect for the government and its laws. We should tell people, in no uncertain terms, that decrees of the government have no moral legitimacy whatever—that they are on par with decrees of the Mafia. We must work to delegitimize and demystify the State. Of course, there is the practical problem of avoiding penalties, and individuals may choose to obey particular laws in order to escape punishment. But a government that must rely entirely on fear cannot long survive. All governments must cloak themselves in legitimacy in order to win the passive acquiescence of their subjects. Libertarians must seek to dissolve this aura of legitimacy. We must tell people: you have certain rights, period; and what the government does cannot change that. The government is a thug and a thief; be on your guard, watch it with caution, for it is powerful. But do not be awed by it. Do not grant it respect or moral sanction. Treat it as you would any villain.

I submit that if this disrespect could be inculcated on a wide scale, we would experience a rebirth of liberty in America. Politicians would be

Should Libertarians Vote or Hold Political Office? (Smith)

63

beside themselves if only one percent of the population showed up to vote. Politics would be a laughing stock. One law after another could be passed, and nobody would pay any attention. The government would die of neglect.

This rather than political action, is the course I would recommend to libertarians. And the likelihood of its success is no less than the prospect of dismantling the government from within. Granted, it lacks the flashy trappings of political campaigns. There would be no campaigns and media hype. It would be a quiet revolution and one that is largely decentralized. It would entail dozens of different strategies. It would take a long time, and it wouldn't be glamorous. There would be few, if any, positions of power to fight for. It would require dedication and knowledge. But it could be deadly.

This strategic vision, as I have argued, is incompatible with political action. We wish people to look elsewhere than government for their freedom. We wish them to view government with contemptuous indifference. This cannot be achieved through political action.

12

Elections Enhance Government Power and Authority

by Benjamin Ginsberg

The Consequences of Consent: Elections, Citizen Control and Popular Acquiescence *(Reading: Addison-Wesley Publishing Company, 1982), pp. 160–164. The author is currently David Bernstein Professor of Political Science at Johns Hopkins University, Baltimore.*

Not only do elections contain and delimit the impact of mass political activity, but they also transform the otherwise sporadic and potentially dangerous political involvement of the masses into a principle source of national power and authority. First, elections bolster popular support for political leaders and for the regime itself. In particular, the formal opportunity to participate can help to convince citizens that the government is responsive to their needs and wishes. Second, elections help to persuade citizens to obey. Electoral participation encourages popular cooperation with the government's programs and policies, particularly popular acquiescence to the taxation and military service upon which the state's existence depends. Electoral participation, especially in the democratic context, has the effect of substituting consent for coercion ⸱s the foundation of the state's power.

Discussions of the possibility of influence through electoral institutions tend to assume that the effects of elections are unidirectional. Elections are presumed to serve solely, albeit imperfectly, as instruments of popular control of officials' conduct. Yet the possibility of influence through elections has more than one dimension. Whatever effect electoral participation has upon the activities of those in power, elections simultaneously afford governments an opportunity to influence their citizens' attitudes

64

and behavior. At least since the nineteenth century, as we noted earlier, governments have attempted to use popular voting to enhance their own authority and legitimacy. Rulers have typically conceived routine mass participation to be a form of co-optation that could potentially increase popular responsiveness to the government's policy initiatives and diminish popular opposition to national authority.[1] The acquisition of popular consent through participation is a basic underpinning of national power and has been a key factor in the growth and development of the modern state.

The emergence and expansion of modern states can, of course, be explained in a variety of different ways. Yet whatever the precise nature of the underlying causes, the fundamental requirement for the construction of nation-states was the extraction of revenues and services from their citizens. Money, labor, and military service were all essential for the creation and maintenance of the armies and bureaucracies that formed the backbone of the state. Without these resources, rulers could neither defend their territorial claims against external foes nor hope to subordinate such internal rivals as the church and the aristocracy.

To put the matter simply, there are two ways in which rulers can acquire revenues and services from their subjects—coercion and persuasion. A populace may be forcibly compelled to provide its rulers with revenues and services or may be persuaded to do so of its own free will. All governments, or course, employ elements of both persuasion and coercion. Generations of American men, for example, were offered a choice between voluntary military enlistment and involuntary conscription. Behind the warm handshake of the genial recruiting sergeant lurked the cold tentacles of the remorseless Selective Service System.

Though coercion and persuasion often complement one another in this way, it was clearly coercion that was the more important factor during the early history of state building. In what Finer characterizes as the extraction-coercion cycle, rulers used force to collect taxes and compel service in the military.[2] The growth of armies and bureaucracies increased

---

[1]*See, for example, Edward Shils,* Political Development in the New States *(Gravenhage: Mouton, 1962); Aristide Zolberg,* Creating Political Order *(Chicago: Rand McNally, 1966); and Richard Rose and Harve Mossawin, "Voting and Elections: A Functional Analysis,"* Political Studies *15 (1967): 173–201. See also Murray Edelman,* The Symbolic Uses of Politics *(Urbana: University of Illinois Press, 1964), and Murray Edelman,* Politics as Symbolic Action *(Chicago: Markham, 1971). See also Easton's concept of "diffuse support" for a regime and political leaders. David Easton,* A Systems Analysis of Political Life *(New York: Wiley, 1965), especially ch. 18. This theme of the use of elections to build popular support runs through all the essays in Guy Hermet, Richard Rose, and Alaine Rouquié (eds.),* Elections Without Choice *(New York: Wiley, 1978). Contrary to the implication of this excellent volume's title, however, elections "without choice" are not the only sorts of voting processes that can be used to increase popular acquiescence.*

rulers' capacity to extract revenues and service, which in turn made possible the construction of larger armies and bureaucracies, and so on. This cycle of extraction and coercion was at the heart of state building in Western Europe. When, for example, Frederick William succeeded as Elector of Brandenburg-Prussia in 1630, he commanded a military force consisting of a mere 1300 mercenary troops, had virtually no central administrative machinery, and was at the mercy of the Estates for revenues. In stages over the next 40 years, Frederick used his troops to acquire more funds, with which he retained more troops, with which he in turn enforced the collection of more taxes. By the conclusion of Frederick William's reign in 1688, Brandenburg-Prussia boasted a standing army of 30,000 men and an elaborate administrative machinery. This cycle was continued by Frederick William I, who was able to construct what on a per capita basis was the largest standing army in Europe. This permanent force of 80,000 troops both supported and was supported by an extensive bureaucracy and tax collection apparatus.[3]

Though it was certainly crucial to the construction of nation-states, ultimately coercion alone is a shaky foundation for governmental power. Coercion tends to engender resistance. And, indeed, resistance was one of the major problems of state-building. Popular resistance to military service, to the expropriation of food and supplies for armies, and above all, to taxation were central themes in European history from the fifteenth century onward. In France, for example, several hundred antitax riots occurred during Richelieu's ministry alone.[4] In Spain, tax increases led to widespread urban rebellion in Castille in 1520.[5] In England, resistance to taxation and other royal demands led to serious rebellions in 1489, 1497, 1536, 1547, 1549, and 1553.[6] Between the fifteenth and eighteenth centuries the questions of how to deal with popular resistance to taxation and service was among the chief preoccupations of European rulers. Even if popular resistance is not sufficient to topple a government or prevent the collection of taxes, opposition can make the costs of extraction very high. The expenditure of resources necessary to extract resources from a recalcitrant population may leave little net gain.

[2] Samuel Finer, "State and Nation Building," in Charles Tilly (ed.), The Formation of National States in Western Europe (Princeton, N.J.: Princeton University Press, 1975), p. 84.

[3] Ibid., pp. 134–144. See also Gordon A. Craig, The Politics of the Prussian Army (New York: Oxford University Press, 1955), ch. 1.

[4] Charles Tilly, "Reflections on the History of European State-Making," in Tilly, Western Europe, especially pp. 22 and 71.

[5] Ibid., p. 22.

[6] Ibid.

Ultimately, states that relied solely upon coercion were unable to compete successfully with those that managed to induce popular cooperation. It was the unprecedented size, ardor, and military success of the citizen armies of postrevolutionary France that provided the first concrete demonstration of the power that could be tapped by enlisting the active cooperation of a populace. The gradual expansion of participation during the remainder of the nineteenth century represented, in large measure, an attempt by other nations to copy the French example and to increase governmental power by harnessing the collective energy of the masses.[7] Again, the slogan coined during the nineteenth-century Swedish suffrage debates, "One man, one vote, one gun," is an excellent illustration of the relationship that was believed to exist between mass participation and the state's power.

The use of elections to enhance governments' power and authority is, of course, most dramatic in the totalitarian context. The "elections without choice" staged by authoritarian regimes are, indeed, pure cases of the use of mass participation to mobilize popular support, intensify mass identification with the state and its goals, and isolate the regime's opponents. Both European Communist and Fascist elections have typically included a good deal of ceremony and festivity. Though the vote may not include a choice, it is, upon occasion, treated as a quasi-religious confession of faith in the regime. For example, the 1933 German ballot asked. "Do you approve, German man, and you, German woman, the policy of your Reich's government and are you ready to declare it as the expression of your own conception of your own will and to confess yourself solemnly for it?"[8] Presumably there could be but one appropriate response.

But even though the overt efforts of authoritarian regimes to obtain mass consent through participation are more heroic and dramatic, over time it is the democratic election that is the more effective source of popular support. Particularly in the context of sophisticated advanced industrial societies, elections without choice tend ultimately to breed cynicism more than they generate support. In the Communist nations of Eastern Europe, for example, few citizens appear to believe that voting is an effective means of participating in political affairs. As a result, several of these regimes have begun to introduce a limited degree of choice in elections at

[7] *The Prussians, in particular, sought to learn from the French example. See Reinhard Bendix,* Kings or People *(Berkeley and Los Angeles: University of California Press, 1978), p. 416: Finer, "Nation Building," p. 163; and Craig,* Prussian Army, *ch 2.*

[8] *Juan J. Linz, "Non-Competitive Elections in Europe," in Hermet, Rose, and Rouquié,* Elections Without Choice, *pp. 36–65.*

the local level in an attempt in increase popular interest and involvement with the voting process.[9]

It is the election with choice, the election that allows at least the appearance of effective mass influence, that at the same time most effectively builds popular support for the regime. It is the democratic election that most readily convinces citizens that the government is responsive to their needs and wishes. And as a result, it is the democratic election that can induce citizens to contribute with a minimum of compulsion what the state might not have been able to take by force alone.

[9]*Alex Pravda, "Elections in Communist Party States," in Hermet, Rose, and Rouquié,* Elections Without Choice, *pp. 169–195. The People's Republic of China also began to introduce a measure of choice in local elections in 1979. According to the Communist party's theoretical journal,* Hunychi, *"the more democratic rights the workers enjoy, the stronger their sense of responsibility becomes." Fox Butterfield, "China Tests Voting for Minor Leaders,"* New York Times, *December 10, 1979.*

13

Voting and the
Slavery Analogy

by Alan Koontz

"Living Slavery and All That," in The Voluntaryist *(No. 17, August 1985, p. 7.) The author's website is http://alumni.umbc.edu/~akoont1/tmh/.*

In various forums, at least since the birth of the LP, Murray Rothbard has invoked what he calls the "slavery analogy," to point up the morality of political voting. The question is: Does the slavery analogy really help in this way?

To begin with, Rothbard's slavery analogy illustrates the nature of the State. The condition of the slaves relative to their master is more or less the same as that of the subjects to the State. The master, by either directly or indirectly (through a foreman) exceeding his natural rights, denies his slaves' natural rights, just as the State denies the natural rights of its subjects by its very, existence.

The condition of the slaves is thus a given before the question of "voting rights" arises. Their condition indicates that they have a ruler regardless of whether or not the slaves can vote. The same is true of the subjects of the State. Suppose, then, that the slaves are granted a choice of, say, two foremen by the master. The slaves may cast ballots to decide which foreman will execute rule over the slaves. The foreman who receives the most votes will be the choice of all slaves. Presumably, the slaves will each choose what he or she thinks is the lesser of the two evils. The situation of the slave thus becomes analogous to that of the subject who has been granted the "right to vote" for his ruler. In light of this slavery analogy, Rothbard asks: What is immoral about choosing the lesser of two evils, if that is the only choice one has under the circumstances?

To answer his question: First of all, the choice is one which affects the lives of others besides the chooser. Using the slave analogy, the vote of each slave isn't just a choice of which foreman will rule that slave, but is a choice of who will rule all of the slaves. Thus each slave that votes is acting in the capacity of the master respecting his slaves. To vote for a foreman is to take part in the process of other people's enslavement. It should be clear, at least to Rothbard, that by voting, the slave in respect to his peers is going as far beyond his or her natural rights as the master (or the foreman) does respecting his or her slaves.

Moreover, the possibility certainly exists in the slavery analogy that not all the slaves may be in agreement as to which of the two foremen is the lesser of the two evils. Most importantly, some or all of the slaves may decide that the lesser of the two evils is still evil and on this basis refuse to vote. In either case, the immorality of voting is quite obvious.

It is also obvious that assuming one only has the choice of the lesser or greater of the two evils in the slavery analogy is begging the question. As Frank Chodorov once asked, in this regard "Under what compulsion are we to make such a choice? Why not pass up both of them?" Indeed there is nothing in the slavery analogy that says the slaves must choose one or the other of the two foremen. By making such a choice the slaves are merely doing yet another thing that the master wants them to do. Instead of choosing either foremen, one or more of the slaves may choose neither. This third choice, also open to the slaves, is a moral one for it doesn't affect coercion towards others unlike voting.

Furthermore, the refusal to vote is a first step toward restoring individual sovereignty. If the slave does what the master wants him or her to do he or she will most assuredly remain a slave. (The master, for example, wouldn't give his or her slaves the "right to vote" if the slaves could thereby become free.) By refusing to vote the slave is not doing what the master wants him or her to do. If most of the slaves refused to vote the master would have to choose the foreman for them. However, the master (and foreman) would then be up against a group that has refused to barter his or her individual sovereignty for the lesser of the two evils the master had originally offered: let alone give it up for nothing. And so would it be for the State that failed to get barely any of its subjects to participate in the electoral process.

In short, the answer to the opening question is: No, on the contrary.

14

Elections: An Alternative to Political Disorder

by Benjamin Ginsberg

The Captive Public: How Mass Opinion Promotes State Power *(New York: Basic Books, 1986), pp. 48–54 and pp. 57–58.*

From Spontaneous Assertion to Routine Expression

Before the nineteenth century, mass opinion was almost exclusively asserted through spontaneous and voluntary means—most typically through riot and disorder. During the 1800s, however, governments began to construct formal avenues for the assertion of mass opinion—representative bodies, elections, and the like—and to train citizens in their use. Whatever the other consequences of these institutions, they did enable regimes to reduce the threat that informal expressions of mass opinion often posed to the political order. The construction of electoral institutions was especially crucial in this regard. In the twentieth century, of course, voting has come to be seen as a normal or typical vehicle for the expression of mass political opinion. But it was not always so. Indeed, if there is any natural or spontaneous form of mass political expression, it is the riot.

The fundamental difference between voting and rioting is that voting is a socialized and institutionalized form of mass political expression. The peasant uprising or urban riot is usually a spontaneous affair, sparked by some particular event or grievance. Though riots may have been commonplace, each was itself a unique event. Where and when disturbances occurred and who took part in them usually depended on a unique pattern of circumstances and spontaneous individual choices. Voting, however, is far from spontaneous. Elections provide routine institutional channels for the expression of demands and grievances. They thus trans-

71

mute what might otherwise take the form of sporadic, citizen-initiated activity into a routine public function. When, where, who, and how individuals participate in elections are matters of public polity rather than questions of spontaneous individual choice. With the advent of the election, control over the agenda for the expression of political opinion passes from the citizen to the state. The most obvious consequence of this change was a diminution of the likelihood of disruption and disorder. By establishing an institutional channel of political activity and habituating citizens to its use, governments reduced the danger that mass political action posed to the established political and social order. Elections contain and channel away potentially violent and disruptive activities and protect the regime's stability.

In principle, of course, citizens in democracies are free to assert whatever demands, opinions, views, and grievances they might have through a variety of means. Americans, for example, may, if they wish, lobby, petition, demonstrate, file suit in court, and so forth. Though there are, of course, some legal impediments to many of these forms of participation, relatively few modes of political expression are directly barred by law. Despite the hypothetical availability of an array of alternatives, though, in practice the participation in American politics of ordinary citizens as opposed to members of elite groups is generally limited to voting and a small number of other electoral activities. It is true that voter turnout in the United States is relatively low. However, when, for one or another reason, ordinary Americans do seek to participate, their participation generally takes the form of voting. Relatively few individuals choose to engage in types of political action not formally a part of the electoral process. Indeed, a large number of citizens have never engaged in any form of political action but voting. The preeminent position of voting and other forms of electoral involvement in the American political process is not surprising, as the American legal and political environment is overwhelmingly weighted in favor of electoral participation generally and voting in particular. Though Americans may in principle do as they wish, members of the mass public are strongly encouraged to participate electorally and to ignore the potential alternatives.

Probably the most influential among the forces helping to channel participants into the electoral arena are law and civic education. For the mere existence of suffrage does not guarantee that citizens will use it in preference to other possible forms of political action. State legislation in the United States not only gives people the vote but prescribes the creation of an elaborate and costly public machinery that makes voting a rather simple task. And civic education, to a large extent legally mandated, encourages citizens to believe that electoral participation is *the* appropriate way to express opinions and grievances. Unlike many other nations, the United States neither obligates its citizens to vote nor prohibits them from engaging in other political activities. Nevertheless, systemic influences facilitate electoral participation, particularly voting, to the near exclusion of other possible forms of political activity.

The Impact of Law

Voting is among the least demanding forms of political involvement. Despite complicating factors such as registration, the time, energy, and effort needed to vote are considerably less than are required by all but a few other political activities. It is, indeed, usually assumed that the relative ease of voting is one of the major reasons why it is more common in the United States than any other mode of participation.

Yet the relatively low degree of individual effort required to vote, however, is somewhat deceptive. The fact of the matter is that voting is simple only because it is made so by an elaborate and costly electoral system. The ease with which citizens can vote is a function of law and public policy rather than an inherent attribute of voting itself. The costs of voting are paid mainly by the state. In the United States electoral contests are administered principally by states and localities, although the Constitution, federal law, and federal court decisions have an obvious bearing on the conduct of elections.

Though state voting is sometimes thought of in terms of regulations and limitations on suffrage, in fact, the bulk of state action in this area is permissive. States must and do create the opportunity to vote before they can begin to regulate it. Indeed, states and localities legally require themselves to invest considerable effort in the facilitating of voting. At the state, county, and municipal levels, boards of elections must be established to supervise the electoral process. For every several hundred voters in each state, special political units—precincts or election districts—are created and staffed exclusively for the administration of elections. During each electoral period polling places must be set up, equipped with voting machines or ballots, and staffed by voting inspectors. Prior to an election, its date, the locations of polling places, and the names of candidates must be publicized. After each election, returns must be canvassed, tallied, reported, and often recounted.

Because virtually all of this activity is borne by municipal governments, the total annual cost of American elections is not known. Even the very spotty evidence that is available, however, suggests that election administration is quite expensive. It is not at all unreasonable to assume that the total annual cost of election administration in the United States is well over $1 billion. This, of course, does not include the enormous cost of campaigns, now partially subsidized by the federal government but which, until recently, was borne entirely by parties, candidates for office, and organized interest groups.

Obviously, in all the states there are selective legal impediments to voting. Age disqualifies some. Registration requirements have an important impact on specific sets of potential voters. Nevertheless, although the laws of every state discourage or disqualify some potential participants, overall the laws diminish the likelihood that citizens will disqualify themselves from voting. Legal facilitation reduces the effort and motivation needed to participate by voting to the point where individuals are less likely to engage in the alternative forms of political action.

Civic Education

Legal facilitation, of course, cannot completely explain the prevalence of voting and the relative absence of alternative forms of mass participation in the United States. If public attitudes were completely unfavorable to elections, it is doubtful that legal facilitation alone would have much impact. The ubiquity of voting, in large part, also reflects generally favorable public beliefs about the electoral process and perhaps a low regard for alternative forms of political action.

Such favorable public attitudes to voting do not come into being spontaneously. As a matter of public policy, Americans are taught to equate participation in politics with electoral participation, and especially with voting. Civic training, designed to give students an appreciation for the American system of government, is a legally required part of the curriculum in every elementary and secondary school and, though it is not as often required by law, civic education usually manages to find its way into college curricula as well.

In the elementary and secondary schools, through formal instruction and, more subtly, through the frequent administration of class and school elections, students are taught the importance of the electoral process. By contrast, little attention is given lawsuits, direct action, organizing, parliamentary procedures, lobbying, or the other possible modes of participation. Obviously the techniques involved in organizing a sit-in or protest march are seldom part of an official school course of study.

The New York State first-grade social studies curriculum offers a fairly typical example of the kind of training in political participation given very young children. The State Education Department provides the following guidelines to teachers:

> To illustrate the voting process, present a situation such as: Chuck and John would both like to be the captain of the kickball team. How will we decide which boy will be the captain? Help the children to understand that the fairest way to choose a captain is by voting.
>
> Write both candidates' names on the chalk board. Pass out slips of paper. Explain to the children that they are to write the name of the boy they would like to have as their captain. Collect and tabulate the results on the chalk board.
>
> Parallel this election to that of the election for the Presidency.
>
> Other situations which would illustrate the election procedure are voting for: a game; an assignment choice; classroom helpers.

Though secondary-school students periodically elect student government representatives rather than classroom helpers and are given more sophisticated illustrations than kickball team elections, the same principle continues to be taught, in compliance with legal requirements. College students are also frequently given the opportunity to elect senators, representatives, and the like to serve on the largely ornamental representative bodies that are to be found at most institutions of higher learning. Millions of college students believe this sort of experience is good preparation for life.

Obviously, civic education is not always completely successful. In the late 1960s and early 1970s sizable numbers of college students and graduates staged sit-ins and demonstrations for various political causes. Segments of the educational process clearly provide skills, resources, and ideas that enable their recipients to participate more readily in a variety of political contexts than those with lower levels of educational attainment. The state's civics curriculum is hardly all that students learn in school. Nevertheless, level of education is strongly associated with interest in elections, belief in the efficacy and importance of voting, and voting itself.

Civic education, of course, does not end with formal schooling. Early training is supplemented by a variety of mechanisms ranging from the official celebration of national holidays to the activities of private patriotic and political organizations. Election campaigns themselves are occasions for the reinforcement of training to vote. Campaigns include a good deal of oratory designed to remind citizens of the importance of voting and the democratic significance of elections. Parties and candidates, even if for selfish reasons, emphasize the value of participation, of "being counted," and the virtues of elections as instruments of popular government. Even though large numbers of Americans stay home on election day, this continuing civic education coupled with legal permissiveness ensures that when Americans do choose to participate they will most always take the electoral route....

Reconstituting Mass Opinion

Thus, over two hundred years, western regimes fundamentally reconstituted mass opinion—changing its modes of formation, its social basis, is political foundations, and its form of expression. When taken together, these four changes amount to a domestication of mass public opinion. Under the pressure of market forces, the solidarity of lower-class opinion was broken; with the development of electoral institutions, the expression of mass opinion because less disruptive; when citizens began to see government as a source of benefits, opinion became fundamentally less hostile to central authority (though not always to particular authorities); with the advent of mass education, governments began to intervene directly in the formation of popular attitudes. In short, western regimes converted mass opinion from a hostile, unpredictable, and often disruptive force into a less dangerous and more tractable phenomenon.

15

The Meaning of Elections

by Benjamin Ginsberg

The Captive Public: How Mass Opinion Promotes State Power *(New York: Basic Books, 1986), pp. 182–186.*

Elections are generally conceived to be the principal means through which ordinary citizens, as distinguished from members of the elite strata (who usually have other means at their disposal), can impose their views upon leaders' conduct. And certainly democratic elections permit citizens to routinely select and depose public officials, and thereby to influence the composition and behavior of the nation's ruling circle. But however effective the electoral sanction may be, it is hardly the only means through which even the most humble citizens can reward or punish public officials for their actions. Spontaneous or privately organized forms of political activity, or even the threat of their occurrence, can also induce those in power to pay attention to their subjects' opinions. The behavior of even the most rigid autocrats, for example, can be influenced by the possibility that their policies may provoke popular disobedience, clandestine movements, or riot and insurrection. To be sure, the likelihood that an autocrat will be removed from office may generally be less than the chance that an elected official will suffer defeat at the polls. At the same time, however, the potential cost of removal via popular insurrection can be significantly greater than the penalties associated with electoral defeat. Though American congressional representatives are occasionally referred to the private practice of law by their constituents thus far at least few have lost their heads. Elections do not create a possibility of popular influence where none existed before. Rather, they substitute an institutional mechanism for the informal sanctions that might otherwise be available to a mass public. Elections transform citizens' capacity to influence their rulers' behavior from a matter of purely private activities and resources to a result of mass participation in a routine public function. This transformation has several critical consequences.

First, elections formalize and thus fundamentally alter the character of popular influence over governments' actions. As I noted earlier, while citizens' opinions could influence public officials long before the advent of elections, in the absence of formal mechanisms for its expression and enforcement, the influence of popular opinion tended to be inversely related to rulers' power. Rulers are likely to be most concerned with their subjects' wishes when their military and administrative capacity to compel obedience or forcibly maintain their positions is weakest and least concerned with citizens' views when their own power is most secure. Popular influence stemming from rulers' fear of disobedience— riot or insurrection, for example—is likely to be greatest when the state's military and internal security forces are weakest or least reliable. The advent of the democratic election, however, meant that even when rulers had the capacity to compel obedience, popular influence was no longer necessarily reduced. Citizens' capacity to influence their rulers' conduct had become at least partially independent of rulers' military and administrative power. The effectiveness of the electoral sanction, unlike that of the threat of riot and insurrection, does not necessarily vary with the state's power. Even the most powerful elected official can be voted out of office. With the advent of the democratic election, popular influence and rulers' power were no longer necessarily inversely related but could instead potentially coexist.

At the same time that they institutionalize the influence of public opinion, however, elections have a second consequence: they delimit popular influence. Elections introduce a means of mass influence that is itself subject to formal governmental control and manipulation. In every nation the electoral rules and procedures that translate individual opinions and choices into collective decisions and determine the impact of those decisions upon the government's composition are used by those in power to regulate electoral outcomes and their likely consequences. Electoral rules can obviously be employed to diminish or even to preclude the possibility of electoral influence. Examples of authoritarian elections without choice are numerous. But even where competition and choice are routine possibilities, election law can play an important role in preserving an established distribution of power. The democracies characteristically do not attempt to prevent mass influence via the ballot box. Instead, electoral law in the democratic context is typically used to organize the expression of mass opinion in such a way that its force is channeled to the advantage of the regime. Rather than prevent mass electoral influence, democracies attempt typically to "influence mass influence," so that the electorate's decisions themselves will accord with and thus reinforce the power and wishes of those who rule.

Third, whatever the precise character of the legal constraints on popular influence through voting, elections inherently limit mass intervention into governmental and political processes. To begin with, elections limit the frequency of citizen participation in politics. In the United States elections occur at fixed points in time and grant elected officials the freedom and authority to govern, without fear of citizen intervention, for a defined term. So long as participation is confined to periodic voting, officials have an opportunity to overlook public sentiment about the conduct of public affairs much of the time.

Moreover, elections limit the scope of mass political participation. Elections permit citizens to take part only in the selection of leaders. The mass public does not directly participate in subsequent policy making. Though there may be links between citizens' choices among candidates for office and choices about the government's actions, elections do not usually function as referenda on issues or policies. Indeed, as we shall see, elections in the United States tend for the most part to focus mass attention exclusively on the question of who shall govern and to divert it away from questions of how and what the government shall do.

Last, elections limit the intensity of mass political activity by converting it from a means of asserting demands to a collective statement of permission. In the absence of formal avenues for popular involvement, political participation serves almost exclusively as a device for the expression of strongly held beliefs and preferences. So long as political involvement is difficult, usually only those individuals with intense or extreme opinions will be sufficiently motivated to seek to become involved. Elections, however, facilitate participation sufficiently that large numbers of citizens take part despite their relative indifference or apathy about most public questions. Just as polls can dilute the weight of those with intense views, elections usually submerge those participants with strongly held views in a generally apathetic mass electorate.

Thus, while elections are usually seen as synonymous with mass political influence, their consequences are not so simple. Elections institutionalize popular influence but can at the same time constrain and delimit the effects of mass intervention into political life. It is undoubtedly true that popular influence through democratic electoral institutions is significantly greater than, say, the influence available to citizens ruled by a dictatorship sufficiently powerful to prevent dissent and disorder. But this comparison, often implicit when the importance of democratic elections is discussed, is not necessarily the most apt. In what at least historically has been the more usual case, governments often have not been powerful enough to stamp out clandestine oppositions or prevent political violence and disorder. And under such circumstances, the influence that the masses have been able to exert through these modes of political expression, or even their threat, has been substantial. The alternative to democratic elections is not clearly and simply the absence of popular influence but can instead be unregulated and unconstrained mass intervention into governmental processes. It is indeed often precisely because spontaneous forms of mass political activity can have too great an impact upon governments' actions that elections are introduced. Distinguished political commentator Walter Lippmann once observed that "new numbers were enfranchised because they had power, and giving them the vote was the least disturbing way of letting them exercise their power." The vote can provide the "least disturbing way" of allowing the masses to exercise power because elections formally delimit mass influence that rulers are unable to forcibly contain. If the masses had no power without them, elections would never have been introduced.

16

The Case
Against Democracy

by Carl Watner

"The Case Against Democracy: The More Things Change, The More They Remain the Same," in The Voluntaryist *(No. 45, August 1990, pp. 3–4). Carl Watner, editor of this book, is an independent scholar and businessman.*

DEMOCRACY. For many, the word sums up what is desirable in human affairs. Democracy, and agitation for it, occurs all over the world: the Pro-Democracy movement in China during 1989; the democratic reform movements taking place in Eastern Europe and the U.S.S.R. resulting in the breakup of the Communist Party's monopoly over electoral activity; and the U.S. invasion of Panama to restore democratic government.

Future historians may label the Twentieth Century as the Age of Democracy. From Woodrow Wilson's salvo, "Make the world safe for democracy," and the ratification of the 19th Amendment (1920) giving women the vote, to a 1989 observation of one Philippine writer—"In the euphoria of the [democratic Aquino] revolution, people expected that with the restoration of democracy all the problems of the country would be solved"—little has changed. Democracy has been hailed as the solution to many political problems. However much we would like to believe in democracy, we still need to recall that democracy is nothing more than a form of statist control. The purpose of this article is to briefly review the history and development of democratic political theory from a voluntaryist perspective, and to explain why the world-wide movements toward democracy (the more things change) do not alter the nature of the State (the more they remain the same).

DEMOCRACY. The word is ultimately traceable to two Greek

roots, referring to "the rule of the common people or populace." As *The American College Dictionary* puts it, democracy is "government by the people; a form of government in which the supreme power is vested in the people and exercised by them or their elected representatives under a free electoral system." In the ancient democracies of Sparta and Athens, every free citizen was entitled to attend legislative assemblies and vote, but not every person was a freeman (slaves, women, and children were denied participation). The modern western democracies of the 19th and 20th Centuries have tended to be based on the assumption of equality of all human beings (though children, convicted felons, and the mentally incompetent may not vote) and upon the idea of representation, where the people elect representatives to conduct the affairs of State.

It is no exaggeration to conclude that the modern concept of democracy has emerged as the result of the age-old search for "the best and most equitable form of government." Most commentators would agree that the essentials of modern democracy, as we know it today, include: 1) "holding elections at regular intervals, open to participation by all political parties, freely administered, where the voting franchise is universal"; and 2) "respect for fundamental human rights, including freedom of expression, freedom of conscience, and freedom of association," based upon the "fundamental assumption of the equality of all individuals and of their equal right to life, liberty, and their pursuit of happiness." It is important to note, at this point, that the advocate of democracy already presupposes that we need a State. By focusing on the less important question of "what kind of government is best," democracy and its spokesmen through the ages have ignored the more fundamental question of "why is any form of the State necessary?"

Why does democracy appear to be the "best form of government?" The answer to this question helps explain its persistence. Ever since political philosophers and politicians have tried to justify the State and the exercise of political power, they have been faced with solving the problem of political obligation. Why should some people obey rules and laws, so called, passed by other people? How do the actions of the legislators bind those who refuse to recognize their authority? By what right do the governors wield force to enforce their edicts? In short, what makes one form of government legitimate and another form not? Defenders of democracy answer these questions by pointing out that the history of democracy is largely the history of the inclusion of more and more people of a given country in the exercise of the ballot. It is through the idea of the right of the people to vote (to govern themselves) that the question of political obligation is answered. George Washington pointed out that, "The very idea of the right and power of the people to establish government presupposes the duty of every individual to obey the established government." By involving the whole community, or as many people as possible, democracy garners support for the "laws" passed in its name by the people's representatives. It does so by creating the theory that all the factions participating in an election agree to accept its outcome. In other words, the minority agree to abide by the decision of the majority in the electoral process. (For a discussion of the riddles of electoral representation see *The Voluntaryist*, No. 30. "Some Critical Considerations of the United States Constitution.")

Why should anyone agree to such an implicit contract? Why should one person, or some group of people, be bound by the outcome of an election—what *other* people think is advisable? The only possible answer is that it is a precondition to participation. But then, why should anyone participate? Democratic theory has never really answered this question because it already assumes that government is a social necessity. The importance of this point is found in the observation that "every ruling group must identify with a principle acceptable to the community as justification for the exercise of [its] power." In other words, if there is to be a ruling class in society, if political power is to be exercised, then the rulers must obtain some sort of sanction from the ruled. Democracy admirably serves this purpose because it focuses on the apparent right of the whole community to share in the direction of State.

As I observed in "The Myth of Political Freedom," the idea of political freedom is a charade. The appearance is that the populace has some say in the direction of its government whereas the reality is that they are being manipulated by a system which has been designed to minimize the effects of their input. If people think that their activities influence the outcome of elections and policy-making, then they are likely to be complacent in abiding by the outcome. In short, this involves a process of co-optation, in which the participants are deluded into thinking that their involvement has a significant effect, whereas in reality it matters very little. The purpose of participation is to focus on "how shall we be ruled?" rather then "should we be ruled?" Democracy has survived and has been the most popular solution to the problem of justifying political authority because it has most successfully and most persuasively kept the political game within this framework.

Events in Eastern Europe and the U.S.S.R. serve to illustrate this thesis. When a ruling class loses or lacks a preponderance of force, or when force no longer serves as a threat to enslavement, the only alternative is to obtain the voluntary compliance of the people through the participatory and representative mechanisms of democracy. Thus a *Wall Street Journal* reporter was able to write on June 7, 1989, that, "Far from undermining the Communist leadership, the Soviet 'democracy' movement has actually strengthened Mr. Gorbachev's political legitimacy,...." Indeed, that is the whole purpose of democracy. As Benjamin Ginsberg in his book *The Consequences of Consent*, has noted:

> [Democratic] institutions are among the most important instruments of governance. Elections set the limit to mass political activity and transform the potentially disruptive energy of the masses into a principal source of national power and authority. Governments, ... rule through electoral institutions even when they are sometimes ruled by them [244].

Thus it is plain to see why the communist systems are ready to accept some form of democracy or "democratic socialism." Democratic institutions are likely to emerge where the public "already possesses—or threatens to acquire—a modicum of freedom from governmental control." As Ginsberg explains, "democratic elections are typically introduced where governments are unable to compel popular acquiescence" (245). Ginsberg theorizes that "elections are inaugurated in order to persuade a resistant populace to surrender at least some of its freedom and allow itself to be governed."

Democratic participation in elections is offered as a substitute for the people's natural freedom. In the days prior to the Constitution, social power in the United States was stronger than or at least equal to political power. The populace could not have been compelled to accept a government it did not desire because there was no military force strong enough to overcome its resistance. Social power not only rested on the bearing of weapons, but on the strength of private associations, churches, and community groups which could be voluntarily organized if the need arose. Several framers of the Constitution urged the adoption of a democratic form of government on the grounds that the people would otherwise refuse to accept the new Constitution. Generally speaking, wherever and whenever rulers lack a clear preponderance of force, they tend to become much more concerned with the acquisition of voluntary compliance through democratic methods. As Ginsberg puts it:

> When sizable segments of the public possess financial, organizational, educational, and other resources that can be used to foment and support

opposition, those in power are more likely to see the merits of seeking to persuade rather than attempting to force their subjects to accept governance [247].... It is, in a sense, where the citizens have the means to maintain or acquire a measure of freedom from governmental authority that they must occasionally be governed through democratic formulas. And it is in this sense that freedom is an historical antecedent of democracy [248].

The rulers in a democracy must obscure the inherent conflict between personal freedom and governmental authority. They do so by largely relying on the electoral mechanism and citizen involvement with government. How, the rulers ask, can a government controlled by its citizens represent a threat to the freedom of those who vote and participate? They do so by consistently ignoring the fact that all government, by its very nature, is arbitrary and coercive. As Sir Robert Filmer asked during the 17th Century, if it be tyranny for one man to govern, why should it not be at least equal tyranny for a multitude of men to govern?

> We flatter ourselves if we hope ever to be governed without an arbitrary power. No: we mistake, the question is not whether there shall be an arbitrary power, whether one man or many? There never was, nor ever can be any people governed without a power of making laws, and every power of making laws must be arbitrary.

To the voluntaryist, a man is still a slave who is required to submit even to the best of laws or the mildest government. Coercion is still coercion regardless of how mildly it is administered. Most everyone (the author included) would prefer to live under a democratic form of government if the choice is between "forms of government," but that is not the point at issue. As Aristotle recognized in his *Politics* (though he was not opposed to it), "The most pure democracy is that which is so called principally from that equality which prevails in it: for this is what the law in that state directs; *that the poor shall be in no greater subjection than the rich*" (emphasis added). From the voluntaryist point of view, neither the rich nor the poor should be under any "subjection" or coercion at all. The search for democracy is like the search for the "fair" tax or "good" government. Due to the nature of the "beast" there can be no such thing. Yet the clamor for democracy has persisted for at least 2500 years. The more things change, the more they remain the same!

17

Do Voting and Residence Imply Consent?

by A. John Simmons

On the Edge of Anarchy *(Princeton: Princeton University Press, 1993), pp. 220–228.*
The excerpts are taken from Chapter 8, "Consent, Obligation, and Anarchy," (8.1 "Con-
sent and Voting," and 8.2 "Consent and Residence"). The author is Commonwealth
Professor of Philosophy at The University of Virginia, Charlottesville.

What is to be made of the claims that voting or continued residence
in a democratic state constitute ways of giving consent? Let me consider
these suggestions in turn, beginning with the view that having or exercising the right to vote establishes that the governed have consented in
an appropriate fashion to legitimate governmental control. This claim is
a familiar feature of liberal democratic rhetoric; and it may be ... an issue
more directly relevant to Locke's thought than is commonly supposed.
First, of course, it makes a difference whether it is claimed that consent
is given by the mere possession of a right to vote, or only by actually exercising that right (i.e., voting). The first, stronger version of the claim (that
mere possession of a right to vote is sufficient) would justify asserting
that *all* citizens in typical democracies are consenters. It is hard to see,
though, how consent could be given simply by having a right; this appears
to conflate with actually consenting. The weaker version of the claim (that
actually voting is what gives consent) initially seems more reasonable. It,
however, faces difficulties of a different sort. In the first place, many citizens in existing democracies fail to vote in particular elections, many vote
in none at all, and very few citizens vote in *all* democratic elections. Presumably, then, some citizens' consent is much more extensive than others', while non-voters cannot be understood to have consented at all. And
one would have to assume that since what is typically voted *for* is a candidate for a political office of limited term, consent is given only to the

authority of that candidate for that term. This seems far short of the over-arching consent to the authority of government that was supposed to be given in the act of voting.

Perhaps this conclusion will incline us away from the weaker claim about voting back toward the stronger. Perhaps the stronger claim is really this: in possessing the right to vote in a democratic society, we possess the power to change laws, alter the Constitution, remove public officials, and so on. Insofar as we do *not* do these things, we can be understood to consent to the authority of the law, constitutional provisions, and political officeholders. Again, this is all familiar enough from the rhetoric of democratic life, but it involves so many confusions that I despair of mentioning them all. It once again involves confusing "going along with" something, or acquiescing in it, with consenting to it. It involves supposing that consent can be given to arrangements (laws, officeholders) of which one may have no knowledge and without intending to consent to anything. *Failing* to do something can only be a way of consenting when that inactivity is in response to a clear choice situation, only when inactivity is significant as indicating that a choice has been made (and, as we will see, not always even then). Inactivity that results from ignorance, habit, inability, or fear will not be a way of consenting to anything. Citizens of modern democracies are not continuously, or even occasionally, presented with situations where their inactivity would represent a clear choice of the status quo.

But I have not yet mentioned the most obvious, and most damaging, shortcomings of the strong claim about voting. Individuals in democratic societies do not possess the right to change laws, constitutional provisions, or public officials. Only majorities possess this right. There is, then, no sense at all in which *my* failure to exercise *my* right to do these things constitutes *my* consent to the status quo. I have no such right. Nor is there any obvious sense in which I have granted the majority the right to act for me in these matters. For that one would need, in any event, a unanimous *prior* consent to majority rule that could not have been given by voting (as in Locke's account of the origin of a legitimate polity...). Majority rule in actual practice, however, is a product not of individual consent but of political convention. There is, of course, a clear sense in which "the people" as a whole or "the body politic" possess a right to alter their political institutions (and the like) in a democratic society. Is the failure of "the people" to accomplish such alterations a sign of the consent of the governed? Claiming that would involve the same confusions that I noted in the individual case. The maxim that "silence (or inactivity generally) gives consent" is a very misleading one. Silence virtually *never* gives consent. It does so only where that silence is a freely chosen response to a clear choice situation. And even if the silence of "the people" did give a kind of consent to democratic institutions, this "consent" in no way translates into the individual consent of particular citizens living in the state.

One final but extremely important point: we would do well to remember that voting is often a way not of consenting to something, but only of *expressing a preference*. If the state gives a group of condemned prisoners the choice of being executed by firing squad or by lethal injection, and all of them vote for the firing squad, we cannot conclude from this that the prisoners thereby consent to being executed by firing squad. They do, of course, choose this option; they approve of it, but only in the sense that they prefer it to their other option. They consent to neither option, despising both. Voting for a candidate in a democratic election sometimes has a depressingly similar structure. The state offers you a choice among candidates (or perhaps it is "the people" who make the offer), and you choose one, hoping to make the best of a bad situation. You thereby express a preference, approve of that candidate (over the others), but consent to the authority of no one.

Those who wish to defend the weaker version of the voting consent thesis in the face of such objections, insist that voting in a democratic election is necessarily a way of consenting because there are clear conventions governing such elections. It is made clear to voters that in casting their ballots they are participating in a political process designed to produce a result that all are morally obligated to accept. You cannot perform the acts that are clearly indications of consent (to the authority of the elected candidate) and then happily argue that you were only expressing a preference, not consenting, any more than a person can say (with a full knowledge of the implications), "I consent to X" and then claim not to have consented to X after all. Certain acts, when performed knowingly, intentionally, and voluntarily, just *are* acts of consent, like it or not.

Is voting in a democratic election such an act? It seems obvious to me that it is not. In the first place, the conventions governing such elections are hardly crystal-clear; one could be forgiven for not understanding the (alleged) moral significance of casting one's ballot. I would guess that average voters have very little sense of what they have committed themselves to by voting. This conjecture, if true, is especially damaging to the argument under consideration; for the more centrally our important interests are involved (as they are in political cases), the clearer our signs of consent must be for them to bind us. But even if I am wrong in my guess, the government *itself* in effect routinely declares in modern democracies that voting is *not* a way of morally binding oneself to the state. For voting is typically portrayed not only as a right, but as a *duty* of citizens, suggesting that the status and duties of citizenship have some entirely different basis than the "consent" given in voting. Nor is it ever suggested that by *not* voting one would be freed of obligations that voters voluntarily assume. In short, the government makes it clear that we should go to the polls and express our preference, but that our political obligations (and its rights over us) in no way depend on this and will be in no way altered by failing to do it. Our conclusion must be that the conventions governing democratic elections, and the rhetoric surrounding them, do not establish that voting is a way of undertaking obligations and granting authority (i.e., a way of consenting in the sense that interests us here). And, of course, if the conventions in this area are not clear on that point, voting simply is not a way of giving consent, unless it is accompanied by some (nonmechanical) further act of consent.

Consent and Residence

Let us turn, then, to the second (Locke's) proposal concerning the consensual basis of a free society: that by continuing to reside in a state that we are free to leave (whether by taking possession of land or not), we give our consent to the authority of its government, as least during our residence. Some nondemocratic (and even quite oppressive) governments, of course, also give their citizens the right to free emigration. So if the consent theorist can defend this thesis, he will either have shown that government by consent is a reality (and hence that government is morally legitimate) in more states than we might initially have expected, or else he will be obliged to defend severe limits on what our consent can bind us to (as in Locke). But it is surely a standard feature (if not a defining characteristic) of democratic societies that they allow such free emigration. So in examining this line of argument we will also be saying something special about the respects in which democratic governments enjoy the consent of the governed.

The view that residence (at least in certain kinds of states) constitutes consent has enjoyed a long history. It was first suggested by Plato in the *Crito*, of course, long before Locke's *Treatises*. Others among the classical contract theorists (such as Hobbes and Rousseau) and many philosophers in this century have agreed with Locke. In *Moral Principles and Political Obligations* [Princeton: Princeton University Press, 1979], I argued against the view that continued residence, even in democratic states, could properly be taken as an act of consent to the authority of government. While my views on the proper conclusion of the argument have not changed significantly, I do believe that the case I presented there was too weak to establish that conclusion. I will try to remedy that defect here.

We must begin with the most general conditions for an act to be an act of binding consent (i.e., for consent to be a clear ground of obligation and right-transfer). Consent must, first, be given knowingly and intentionally. Second, binding consent must be given voluntarily. Consent can ground obligations only when it is freely given and adequately informed. These requirements apply, I will suggest, even where the alleged consent is (as in the case of continued residence) tacit only. Let me take these requirements separately, beginning with the requirement that binding consent be given knowingly and intentionally.

Where an apparent consenter has tried to do something other than consent (or tried to do nothing at all), or where, as a result of incapacity, ignorance, confusion, or fraud, he does not fully comprehend what he is taken to have consented to, there is no (or only appropriately circumscribed) binding consent. When the (very) confused foreigner, speaking (very) little English, tries to order a pound of bologna with the words, "I consent to your authority over me," he has consented to nothing. Only when the appropriate words, actions, or inaction are intentionally utilized with awareness of their significance can binding consent be given.

This seems to be taken for granted in the following passage from Hume's essay ["Of the Original Contract." In Hume's *Ethical Writings*. Ed. A. MacIntyre. London: Collier, 1970]: "It is strange that an act of the mind, which every individual is supposed to have formed, and after he came to the use of reason, too, otherwise it could have no authority; that this act, I say, should be so much unknown to all of them, that over the face of the whole earth, there scarcely remain any traces or memory of it."

Here Hume insists that consent is "an act of the mind," by which we may (charitably) understand him to mean that consent must be an intentional act, undertaken with reasonably full awareness of its significance and consequences. Where there is no awareness of having consented, no consent has been given. If Hume is right in this claim, then he is also right that the honest testimony of each of us will ultimately determine whether we have consented to our governments' authority (assuming only that our memories are accurate). And if we further accept, as I believe we should, that very few ordinary citizens are aware of ever having given consent to their governments' actions, this will count heavily against the "generality" of consent theory's account of political obligation and authority. Hume applies the point thus, in his challenge to the view that residence gives consent:

> Should it be said, that, by living under the dominion of a prince which one might leave, every individual has given a tacit consent to his authority, and promised his obedience; it may be answered, that such an implied consent can only have place where a man imagines that the matter depends on his choice. But where he thinks (as all mankind do who are born under established governments) that by his birth, he owes allegiance to a certain prince or a certain form of government; it would be absurd to infer a consent or choice, which he expressly, in this case, renounces and disclaims.

Continued residence cannot be taken to ground political obligation unless residence is understood to be one possible choice in a mandatory decision process. Residence must be seen as the result of a morally significant choice. It is not enough that the choice is available; it must be understood by each person to be a required choice, with mere residence not constituting, for instance, a way of declining to choose. And in Hume's view, of course, these conditions are not satisfied in our actual political lives. Residence requires no "act of the mind" as consent does.

To the consent theorist inclined to try to avoid this conclusion by *denying* that binding consent must be knowingly and intentionally given, it seems sufficient to point out that consent theory is in fact committed to *accepting* this requirement. As we have already seen in the case of Locke, the consent of which the consent theorist speaks must be consent knowingly and intentionally given, for several reasons. First, the consent theorist is attempting to utilize in his work a plausible theory of obligation; the consent with which he concerns himself must be a clear ground of obligation. But surely it is only consent that is intentionally given that satisfies this condition. Consent in any looser, wider sense would be a considerably less convincing example of an obligation-generating act; where the "consent" is given unknowingly, its moral significance becomes extremely doubtful. Second, the most basic point of consent theory, we should remember, has historically been to advance an account of political obligation that is consistent with our intuitive conviction that political bonds cannot be forced on any individual, or fall upon him against his will. Political allegiance is to be a matter for each person's decision, for each is naturally free, with strong rights of self-government (the central thesis of any political voluntarism, like Locke's). Authority exercised over subjects without their permission is illegitimate. But if this ideal of a "free choice" is to be given more than mere lip service, the consent that legitimates political authority must be knowingly and intentionally given. Only the satisfaction of this condition will guarantee that a genuine decision has been made, and a consent theory that recognizes other sorts of consent as binding will undermine its own intuitive support.

We can understand Hume's argument, then, to have two points. It can be seen first as an attack specifically aimed at Locke. For when Locke claims that mere residence in a state constitutes consent to its authority, he seems to allow the possibility that we can give binding consent unknowingly, by merely going about our business. And Hume surely saw this as a case of Locke's sacrificing at once the plausibility and the integrity of his consent theory (and not, as I have urged, as a case of Locke's illegitimately extending the term "consent" to cover the grounds of nonconsensual special obligations). But the broader point of Hume's argument challenges any consent theory, not only Locke's. For if the consent theorist must insist on the intentionality of binding consent, as we have argued, then the consent of ordinary citizens cannot be a subtle process of which "people take no notice ... thinking it not done at all" (II,117). The act that binds us to our political community cannot be one whose true significance is unknown to the actor. Even the person of less than average intelligence must know that he consents when he does so. Hume's simple point, then, seems to strike home. If there is no widespread awareness of the process of political consent, consent theory's account of political obligation cannot have the wide application its proponents have supposed.

18

An Argument in Defense
of the Invisible Hand

by John Pugsley

"Introduction to the 1996 Edition" of Sy Leon's None of the Above *(San Francisco: Fox & Wilkes, 1996), pp. 1–12. Excerpts from "An Open Letter to Harry Browne from John Pugsley: Harry, Please Don't Run for President," appearing in* The Voluntaryist *(No. 74, June 1995) were inserted near the end of this selection with the author's permission. John Pugsley is a financial consultant and author.*

The goal of all individuals of goodwill today and for most of history is and has been individual liberty—the opportunity to work where we want, keep what we earn and pursue the activities we enjoy. The brightest minds of every generation in almost all nations in recorded history have searched for the path to that goal. The discovery of how to achieve freedom has been, and is, mankind's most important quest.

Mankind has clearly failed. Nowhere on earth does man live in anything approaching freedom. Even in the United States, supposedly the "land of the free," the erosion of individual rights has become endemic. The power of the state to tax, regulate and control the lives of citizens seems to constantly grow.

Freedom is the goal, yet after thousands of years of recorded history and thousands upon thousands of tries at creating systems of government that might achieve freedom for individuals, the goal has not been reached.

Why?

It has failed because those searching for a social technology that would ensure individual freedom have incorrectly assumed that freedom could only exist if we first designed the perfect form of government. Even those enlightened geniuses whom we call our "founding fathers" started from the premise that a society can only function if individuals subordinate themselves to a political authority. Outside of a relative handful of libertarians in the world, this belief that men cannot live in harmony without government is nearly universal.

A growing number of individuals are beginning to recognize the wolf in grandmother's nightgown. Government the protector always becomes government the aggressor. Today, thinking people are becoming aware that each time grandmother kisses them, they wind up with a nasty bite. As government grows, the victims multiply.

The common issue facing all freedom-seeking individuals is, how can the cancerous growth of the state be stopped? What can we as individuals do to reverse the trend toward omnipotent government and ultimately achieve the maximum degree of individual freedom?

The two common strategies used down through history to fight back against oppressive government have been either to overthrow tyrants by violent revolution, or to oust them through the democratic process of voting. Unfortunately, violent revolution in most cases replaces one group of tyrants with another, leaving individuals still dominated by government.

The other strategy is to use the electoral process to take control of the state. Those who choose this strategy believe that through voter education, political campaigning and the voting booth, political power can be wrested from special interests, spend-thrift politicians can be excised from government, and the state can be subdued. However, the evidence of history suggests that changing governments in the voting booth has only a modestly better short-term record than violent revolution, and in the long run, individuals are still dominated by oppressive government.

In most people's minds, revolution and voting are the only options for achieving freedom. They are wrong. There is another strategy. Unfortunately, it is so contrary to our cultural indoctrination that only a few in society have the courage to consider it, let alone to stand up against popular opinion and argue its case. This strategy rests on the premise that no other individual, whether that person elects himself by force, or pretends to have authority over you because the majority of your neighbors appointed him, has the right or justification to control your life or property.

It is my belief that a social compact in which each and every individual is free to control his life and property is the only system that can survive in perpetuity. By definition, this means a social system that abandons the right of the majority or the minority to rule. It is a system of self-rule and individual sovereignty.

Those who believe in the principle that the individual should be sovereign refuse to condone political action even as a means to an end. They reject all forms of it. They do not campaign for or against candidates. They do not contribute to political parties or political action committees. They do not write letters to congressmen or presidents. They do not register. And finally, they do not vote. They simply refuse to condone the process of majority rule. It is this almost taboo concept that is addressed in the pages of this delightful book.

Many who believe that majority rule is wrong and destructive still argue that it is necessary to vote in self defense. They believe that by voting for candidates that will promise to reduce the size of government, reduce taxes and reduce regulation, the growth of government aggression can be slowed. And, after all, self defense is moral.

Is voting moral if done in self defense?

Substitute "aggression" for "voting" and the question is more properly stated as, "If aggression were an act of self defense, would it be moral?" Well, something can't simultaneously be moral and not moral. The proper question is, "Am I justified in aggressing against B in order to defend myself from aggression by A?" While aggression in the name of self defense is widely accepted, I'm not certain the argument stands up under scrutiny. If a lion is about to attack our group, can others in the group vote to throw me to the lion and claim that it's an act of self defense? If the mugger tells you he's stealing your money to defend himself against his neighbor, or hunger, or illness, does that make his theft morally acceptable?

In spite of the moral arguments, you may still argue that although it might be immoral to vote, if a minor violation of principle could result in a free world, it would be rational to vote. Even though it violates morality, even though political action may be wrong on some ideological level, why don't we just give it a try? What do we have to lose?

Those who are swayed toward political action have forgotten that we have given it a try. It has been tried for thousands of years in thousands of nations, in tens of thousands of elections and through hundreds of thousands of political parties and candidates. Even if political action only had one chance in 100,000 of resulting in a free nation, statistical probability alone would suggest that there would be at least one free nation today. Mankind has reached the brink of self-extinction giving politics a try.

All of political history can be summed up as a struggle to throw the bad guys out and put the good guys in. Just as Sisyphus was condemned to spend eternity in Hades rolling a rock up a hill only to have it roll down again, so the human race seems to be sentenced to spend forever trying to put the good guys in office only to find they turn bad once there. I'm sorry to say, but when it comes to placing power in the hands of humans, there are no good guys. Thus, the most obvious, and therefore most overlooked reason to eschew political action is that it simply doesn't work.

When you talk to the average person about the advantages of a stateless society, the quick retort is that such an idea is utopian; it would never work. Government is required to control man's selfish nature.

Clearly, the truth is precisely the opposite.

Because of the selfish nature of man, it is utopian to give a human being authority over the lives and property of strangers and to expect that person not to consider his or her own well-being first. Because man is genetically programmed to be self-interested, when one man is placed in a position of authority over another, his natural, genetic impulse is to use that authority to his own advantage. Truly, it is utopian to imagine that a government composed of a small number of individuals would consider the well-being of the general population before considering its own. Behind every law passed by politicians, some politician or political supporter benefited. Lord Acton's famous maxim, "Power tends to corrupt and absolute power corrupts absolutely," perfectly describes the history of government. It does so because it is an astute observation about the nature of man.

If you reject the pragmatic arguments, the moral arguments and the scientific evidence that indicates political action must fail because of the nature of man, there is still a compelling and overriding reason to abandon political action.

On a practical and immediate level, political action is always destructive. I once published "Pugsley's First Law of Government." It was: "All government programs accomplish the opposite of what they are designed to achieve." It is a logical corollary that the same is true of political action.

Consistently down through history, all efforts to put the "good guy" in power have resulted in more government, not less—even when the person elected was expressly elected to reduce the size of government. Let us not forget the mood in the United States when Ronald Reagan first ran for president. Here was a popular hero, a man of the people, who rode into Washington on a white horse. His campaign was simple and directly to the point: government was too big, it was taxing too much, it was spending too much, it was strangling the economy with regulations, and it was no longer a servant of the people. His mandate from the American people was clear: balance the federal budget and reduce the size of the federal government.

What was the result?

In 1980 federal spending totaled $613 billion. In 1988, at the end of Ronald Reagan's tenure, it totaled $1,109 billion. In 1980 federal tax revenue was $553 billion. In 1988 it was $972 billion. Total government debt went from $877 billion to $2,661 billion. Then, to prove the ultimate futility of electing a white knight, the electorate decided that the government wasn't doing enough so it put a liberal democrat back in office. All of the rhetoric of the Reagan campaign is forgotten. All of the public anger over the bureaucracy is forgotten. Government is bigger than ever.

The freedom seeker's involvement in politics always will achieve the opposite of the result intended. No matter who the candidate is or what issues motivate him, political action will not reduce state power; it will enhance state power.

Support of political action strengthens the institution of voting. It plays right into the hands of the constituencies that feed on state power—businesses that gain market share through regulations, laws and subsidies; trade unions that depend for survival on coercive labor laws; entitlement recipients who demand their subsidies; welfare recipients; government employees—all are absolutely dependent on the survival of the myth that "you must get out and vote." In the end there will always be more votes for subsidy than voters who will vote to avoid taxes. There will always be more people struggling to get up to the feeding trough than there will be people determined to keep them away. That is simply human nature.

History does not support the hypothesis that electoral politics might lead to a freer society. There is no case of which I am aware where electoral politics has reduced the size and scope of government in a fundamental or lasting sense. Fundamental reductions seem to have come only on the heels of trauma. Wars, depressions or the outright failure of the state have, on occasions, led to dramatic contractions of state power, the recent collapse of the Soviet Union being an example. But none of these failure-induced contractions can be traced to electoral politics.

The closest thing to victory that history provides as evidence that political action can be used to control the expansion of the state are the tiny and short-lived slowing of government growth such as happened under Margaret Thatcher in England or in recent years under Finance Minister Roger Douglas in New Zealand. But inevitably, the relief is brief and has never resulted in a continuing erosion of state power. Electoral politics has never succeeded in achieving a free society. So, to all of the other arguments against political action, you can add the evidence of history.

In the end, no matter how forceful, how principled or how scientific the arguments presented, you may say, "Principle and reason be hanged, we have to do something!" You may argue that we can't just stand helplessly by and let the politicians have their way with us. Even if it is immoral, even if it is contrary to man's nature, even if in the long run it is counterproductive, and even if there is no evidence that political action has ever been productive, we have to do something. After all, as one pundit once said, "The only thing necessary for the triumph of evil is for good men to do nothing."

This idea, that something must be done, is a disaster. History is replete with instances in which well-meaning people, intent on doing something, turned their discomfort into catastrophe. In past centuries, doctors, ignorant of causes of many ailments but wanting to do something for their patients, commonly bled them, making a sick patient even sicker. Obstetricians in the mid-nineteenth century, not understanding the cause of "puerperal fever" but eager to do something to stop the fatal disease, gave unsanitary pelvic examinations that spread death from patient to patient. When the Black Plague swept Europe in the fourteenth century, people didn't understand the cause, but in their desire to "do something" they killed the cats and burned the witches.

However, the first rule of medicine is, as Hippocrates said, "at least do no harm." Unless you know that the action you are undertaking is right you're much better off doing absolutely nothing....

Fortunately, doing nothing is far from the only alternative to political action. What positive steps can we take? The energy that is now expended by well-intentioned, freedom-seeking individuals on the destructive course of politics can be turned into powerful steps that will have a positive effect on the future. All are moral, right and just. None require aggressing against your neighbor. None require you to abandon principle. Consider the following.

1. *Improve yourself.* Perhaps the single most important thing a person can do (before he sets out to improve others) is to improve himself. Become a model citizen. Don't use government to attack your neighbor, even if you don't like his dog or the color of his house or the color of his skin. If you want to stop others from aggressing through the political process, start by excising from your own life all vestiges of comfort and support for political aggression.

2. *Stop subsidizing your enemy.* Stop loaning the government money. Stop thinking you're profiting by getting a safer return. You wouldn't loan money to your local car thief to see him through a dry spell. Why would

you loan it to the thugs in Washington or Sacramento? Moreover, point out to others that buying T-bills is supporting the muggers and mass murderers in Washington. Pull the drapes back and expose these criminals to the light of day.

3. *Stop doing business with your enemy.* Don't provide products to the government. Don't accept government contracts. Don't do business with government employees. Don't cash government checks—with the possible exception of tax refunds. If you're in business, don't cash them for your customers. Don't take government money. Don't take government subsidies. Don't be a willing, eager beneficiary of political theft.

4. *Stop doing business with people who support your enemy.* Boycott businesses that live on government contracts. Boycott those who lobby for protective legislation. Tell them you don't approve of them stealing from you through the state.

5. *Support private alternatives to government services.* Wherever you can use a private service instead of a government service, use it. Use faxes instead of the Post Office. Use private libraries instead of public ones. Use private schools instead of public schools.

6. *Create parallel mechanisms to replace government functions.* A positive step for society is to show that private enterprise is the correct alternative to government monopolies. By creating Federal Express, Fred Smith did more to reveal the insanity of a government mail monopoly than all of the free market politicians who have ever argued for private mail service on the floors of congress. Most individuals will never understand that all services are best provided by the free market. They do not need to understand the philosophical or intellectual basis for this truth. All they need to do is be given the opportunity to use one or the other. Most of the people who use Federal Express don't understand that it is superior to the government service because it is operated for a profit and not by coercion. They just know it works. Spend your creative energies developing products that compete with government. Put it out of business by offering consumers a better product. Think of all of the things we are told government must do. Develop better home, neighborhood and personal defense services, better consumer protection ideas, safer money, more secure retirement plans, better educational opportunities. With the government absorbing more and more of the private sector, the opportunities for successful private competition are exploding.

7. *Expose the enemy among us.* Instead of talking your neighbors into voting, spend your energy explaining why the political process is their enemy. Talk to centers of influence. Identify the real culprit as the indi-

vidual who promotes bigger government by secretly lobbying for subsidy or privilege. Expose the businessman who is lobbying for a protective tariff, the defense contractor lobbying for tax dollars, the individual seeking government handouts. Call them what they are, mooches and thieves. Embarrass them. Shame them.

8. *Master the issues.* Libertarians should master the issues and learn to communicate so they can explain and persuade others.... Teach others how to confront the irrational arguments of government advocates.

9. *Have the moral courage to confront others.* When somebody makes a statement like, "I'm not in favor of government medicine, but we do have to do something to help the poor," or "even if there are abuses, legalizing drugs is not a serious alternative—we have to enforce the drug laws," libertarians should never sanction such status propaganda by silence.

10. *Get involved in campaigns designed to enlighten and enrage the public.* Speak out against victimless crimes. Support organizations such as The National Taxpayer's Union, Amnesty International, the Fully Informed Jury Association (FIJA) and Families Against Mandatory Minimums (FAMM). Work with groups that are working against regulations. Put pressure on those who are supporting government intrusion. But don't get involved in electoral politics. Don't fight crime by becoming a criminal.

11. *Engage in civil disobedience if you are prepared for the consequences.* Henry David Thoreau went to jail for refusing to pay a small poll tax. He believed that civil disobedience was a moral obligation. His view of political action as a means of changing government was succinctly stated in his tract, *On the Duty of Civil Disobedience.* "How does it become a man to behave toward this American government today? I answer that he cannot without disgrace be associated with it."

12. *Find ways to avoid taxes.* Cut every corner. Make life miserable for a tax collector. Consider using trusts, foundations, tax deferred investments and offshore charities. Your success will be emulated by others, and every dollar denied a thief makes him that much more likely to find another line of work.

13. *Pamphleteer.* Follow the noble lead of Thomas Paine and Lysander Spooner. Tell it like it is. Inundate the talk shows, newspapers and magazines with rational arguments against government. Let other people who are fed up with Big Brother know they are not alone. But show them there is another way than voting.

14. *Write free-market novels and produce free-market movies.* Support companies and individuals that bring a positive message to the audience.

Atlas Shrugged may have had more influence on the direction of freedom today than all the libertarian political activity since it was written.

15. *Consider becoming an expatriate.* Stop falling for the ridiculous cultural blather that says, "my country, right or wrong." Just because you're born at a place controlled by a particular group of politicians doesn't mean they are right. There may be places in the world where you can live in greater freedom than in the U.S. Find them. Vote with your feet....

Political action is built on exactly the same false premise as that of a centrally-planned economy: i.e., that an organized group of political activists engaged in a planned group effort can build freedom more rapidly or better than the individual efforts of independently acting people adhering to the principles of free-market economics as outlined in the works of such giants as Adam Smith and Ludwig Von Mises. The central theme in their economic philosophy is that the "invisible hand" of the market-place—the individual efforts of independently acting people—creates progress and plenty; that any attempt to "organize" and "centrally-plan" economic activity subverts progress and eventually leads to tyranny.

If all the energies now being expended on political action by freedom advocates around the world were focused instead on finding individual solutions, on allowing the "invisible hand" free reign, we would marvel at the ideas and mechanisms that would be bound to evolve.

19

Election Day:
A Means of State Control

by Robert Weissberg

Chronicles, *November 1996, pp. 11–13. Reprinted by permission of* Chronicles, *which is published by The Rockford Institute, 934 North Main Street, Rockford, IL 61103. This article was also reprinted in* The Voluntaryist *(No. 89, December 1997), pp. 1 and 6–7. The author is a professor of political science at the University of Illinois at Urbana-Champaign.*

Interpreting elections is a national spectator sport, offering as many "meanings" as there are board-certified spin doctors. Nevertheless, all of these disparate revelations, insights, and brilliant interpretations share a common, unthinking vision: elections, despite their divisive, contentious character, exist to facilitate citizen power over government. Whether ineptly or adeptly, honestly or dishonestly, government is supposed to be subjugated via mass electoral participation. This is, it might be said, The Great Democratic Belief of Popular Sovereignty.

Less understood, though hardly less significant, is that control flows the opposite way: elections permit government's effective management of its own citizens. The modern state's authority, its vast extractive capacity, its ability to wage war, its ever-growing power to regulate our lives, requires constant reinvigoration via the ballot box. Moreover, and even less obvious, properly administered elections promote cohesiveness, not acrimonious division. Indeed, this periodic reaffirmation of the political covenant may be elections' paramount purpose, relegating the actual choice among Tweedledee, Tweedledum candidates to mere historical details. Like the atmosphere, this phenomenon appears nearly invisible, escaping both popular attention and scrutiny from talking-head television pundits. Even scholars, those investigating civic matters of profound obscurity, with few exceptions (particularly my former colleague, Ben Ginsberg) are neglectful. Put succinctly, marching citizens off to vote—independent of their choice—is a form of conscription to the political status quo. Election day, like Christmas or Yom Kippur, is the high holiday, a day of homage and reaffirmation, in the creed of the modern state.

Those at the Constitutional Convention well understood this conscriptive function. Though the Founders are now fashionably branded as unrepresentative elitists who distrusted the downtrodden masses and oppressed women and toilers of color, what they never doubted was the political usefulness of elections. James Wilson and Elbridge Gerry openly acknowledged that a vigorous federal government required extensive popular consent, freely given by the ballot. Voters could not, and should not, guide policy, but without periodic popular authorization, how could the national government efficiently collect taxes, compel obedience to its laws, solicit military recruits or gain loyalty? This is what "no taxation without representation" is all about: the ritual of consent. Elections, however tumultuous or corrupt, bestowed legitimacy far better and more cheaply than brute force, bribery, appeals to divine right, or any alternative. Opposition to the direct elections of senators, predictably, arose from state sovereignty advocates—allowing citizens to vote for such a prominent national office could only enhance centralism.

Elections as a means of state aggrandizement, not popular control of government, was clearly grasped during the 19th century's march toward universal suffrage. Today's liberal vision of common folk clamoring "empowerment" via the vote is much overdrawn; extension of the suffrage was often "topdown." The modern, centralized bureaucratic state and plebiscitary elections are, by necessity, intimately connected. To Napoleon III and Bismarck the freshly enfranchised voter was the compliant participant in their push toward unified state authority. Casting the national ballot liberated ordinary citizens from the influences of competitors—the church, provincial notables, kinfolk, and champions of localism. Elections soon became essential ceremonies of national civic induction, a process ever-further extended as wars evolved into expensive million-man national crusades.

Modern dictatorships are especially taken with elections, typically combined with some form of compulsory voting, as means of state domination. The Soviet Union's notorious single-party elections with 99+ percent turnout are the paradigmatic but hardly unique example. Many African nations boast of near unanimous turnout to endorse their beloved kleptocratic leader. The Pinochet government of Chile even went so far as to make nonvoting punishable by three months in prison and a $150 fine. While it is tempting to dismiss such choice-less, forced-march elections as shams, the investment of precious state funds and bureaucratic effort confirms that elections are far more than mechanisms of citizen control of government.

In general, the electoral process, whether in a democracy or a dictatorship, performs this citizen domestication function in various ways, but let us examine here only three mechanisms. To be sure, the connection between state aggrandizement and elections is not guaranteed, and much can go astray. Nevertheless, over time the two go together. The first mechanism might be called psychological co-optation via participation: I take part, cast my vote, therefore I am implicated. All of us have been "victims" of the technique beginning, no doubt, as children. Recall, for example, when mom wished your acquiescence to visit hated Aunt Nelly. Despotically demanding compliance, though possible in principle, was too costly. Instead, mom "democratically" discussed alternatives with you, including cleaning house or going to the ballet. Given such choices, you "freely" opted for visiting Nelly, and your subsequent complaints were easily met with "you freely decided."

Such co-optive manipulation extends beyond devious parenting; it is the essence of modern management psychology. Beginning in the 1920s, industrial psychologists realized that "worker involvement" (usually) gained cooperation, especially when confronting unpleasant choices. Let workers conspicuously offer their "input" and they will be far more malleable. Internal "selling" to oneself flows from public choice. Personal participation need not even occur—it is the formal opportunity to add one's two cents, or the involvement of others, that is important. Provided executives define the range of options and control decision-making rules, the "worker empowerment" benefits, not subverts, management. That manipulative inclusion can be labeled "democratic" and "enlightened" and flatters "worker insight" is wonderful public-relations icing on the cake.

This process applies equally to elections. Recall the 1968 presidential contest—a highly divisive three-way race of Hubert Humphrey, Richard Nixon, and George Wallace in which the winner failed to gain a popular majority. Nevertheless, despite all the divisiveness, Ben Ginsberg and I discovered that views of national government, its responsiveness and concern for citizens, became more favorable following the election among voters that among nonvoters. This was also true among those choosing losing candidates. Involvement transcended and overpowered the disappointment of losing. Even a nasty, somewhat inconclusive campaign "juiced" citizen support for government. The pattern is not unique—the election ceremony improves the popularity of leaders and institutions regardless of voting choice.

Elections are also exercises in "Little Leagueism" to help prop up the political status quo. That is, potentially dangerous malcontents are involved in safe, organized activity under responsible adult supervision rather than off secretly playing by themselves. All things considered, better to have Lenin get out the vote, solicit funds, ponder polls, circulate petitions, or serve in Congress. This is equally true in democracies or dictatorships—regular electoral activity facilitates "conventionality" (regardless of ideology) among those who might otherwise drift to the dangerous, revolutionary edge. This is especially true where bizarre groups overall constitute a relatively small minority. At a minimum, humdrum details and ceaseless busy work hardly leaves any time for sitting around a cafe plotting revolution.

Even if all potential revolutionaries are not "domesticated" via the election process, the easy availability of elections helps keep the peace. Why risk mayhem when public employment by stuffing ballot boxes is so simple? The 1960s Black Power movement is the perfect poster child. The urban guerrilla movement back then seemed imminent—the infatuation with Franz Fanon's celebration of violence and similar mumbo-jumbo rhetoric, the macho allure of automatic weapons, and the gleeful "in-your-face" public paramilitarism demeanor. Urban riots were everywhere; Newark and Detroit had become virtual garrison states. Comparisons with Northern Ireland or Lebanon were not absurd.

Nevertheless, the pedestrian seduction of public office easily overcame this intoxication with violence. The Malcolm X Democratic Club and similar entities suddenly materialized while numerous cleaned-up revolutionary agitators entered "the system" as "progressive Democrats," often occupying positions set aside for minorities. The "Black Mayor" became institutionalized. The passage of the 1965 Voting Rights Act, its extensions, and generous subsequent interpretations made black electoral mobilization a national government priority. The federal registrar served as the neighborhood convenience store for " selling out." Within a decade, the once-familiar "revolutionary" agitator spewing forth cliches about insurrection was a political antique. By the 1980s, it was impossible for a "take-to-the-hills" Black Power revolutionary even to think about competing with elections.

The transformation of revolutionary "Black Power" into humdrum conventionality highlights the third way elections domesticate potential disruption: tangible inducement (or bribery, in plain English) to malcontents. The "cooling out" via granting a piece of the action is a time-honored American tradition, from 19th-century populists and socialists to the 1960s antiwar movement. Entering "the system," at least in highly permeable American politics, wonderfully corrupts revolutionary ardor. At a minimum, rabble-rousers in remission must come out of hiding to collect their salary, sit in their offices, boss around subordinates, issue press releases, accept financial contributions, and, if necessary, bounce a check. If Maxine Waters (D-CA) seems like an out-of-control ballistic missile, imagine her unchecked by the obligations of high public office. As a comfortable congresswoman, she is far more constrained than if preaching the street-corner revolutionary gospel or a tenured professor with an endowed chair. Ditto for the thousands of others contemplating revolutionary violence but who now owe their prestige and income to elective office. Let the most ambitious attend endless dull committee meetings. The very existence of this electoral opportunity, apart from bodies enrolled, is critical—the prospect of a few well-paid prestigious sinecures, like playing for the NBA, can work wonders on millions.

This relationship between rising electoral involvement and the demise of 1960s-style revolutionary radicalism helps to explain our collective blind eye toward the extensive corruption in "minority politics." Why do the Protectors of Democracy, from the ACLU to Common Cause, seem so unconcerned with racial gerrymandering, districts comprised largely of illegal aliens, abuses of absentee ballots, outright selling of votes and other nefarious customs when such practices bring blacks and Hispanics to office? More must be involved than just having Third World standards. The answer is simple, though seldom articulated: rotten boroughs, our version of autonomous homelands, are part of the bargain to guarantee domestic peace. The actual outcome is irrelevant; what is important is that up-and-comers, would-be "community leaders," are brought into "the system." Fundamentally, shipping a few dozen would-be agitators off to legislatures or city councils, even felons and dope addicts, hardly puts the national enterprise at serious risk; consider it midnight basketball for the civic-minded. If Washington, D.C., can "survive" Marion Barry, the entire nation is bulletproof.

Elections are but one of many tools of social control and, as with all tools, mere use does not guarantee success. Critical details of administration and organization must be attended to—matters of timing, suffrage, modest enforcement of anticorruption laws, countervailing power within government, and so on. Nor do elections come with an unlimited lifetime warranty to remedy deep political problems. It is doubtful whether elections would solve much in Bosnia or Rwanda, while the jury is still out for Russia and South Africa. Elections are wondrous, circuitous devices, but not all-powerful magic.

Having described this little understood but critical purpose, what lessons can be learned? Two in particular stand out. Most evidently, if one wishes to maintain one's ideological purity, remain uncontaminated in the quest for a higher truth, avoid elections. Those seeking to transform society via "playing the game" will inevitably be metamorphosed by the game itself. This lesson should be heeded by everyone from fundamentalist religious groups to those promoting the redistribution of political power in the United States. Purity and empowerment via elections do not mix. The loss of revolutionary zeal among the formerly faithful, an inclination toward "wheeling and dealing," and being comfortable with petty enticements need not result from flawed character; pedestrian opportunism comes with the territory. If this seems farfetched, one only has to review our history: virtually every splinter group, no matter how ideologically noble or distinct, that ventured into the electoral arena, has been mainstreamed and today exists only as a domesticated, digested fragment within the Democratic or Republican parties.

The surrender of purity via electoral absorption need not, despite advice to the contrary, be a particularly good deal. There are costs, and no guarantee of gain, for getting into bed with the state. You might even get a serious rash. Groups that have devoted themselves extensively to electoral achievement, especially for economic advancement, have seldom, if ever, accomplished much beyond politics itself. This has surely been the case with black infatuation with electoral success since the mid-1960s. Despite all the voting rights laws, federal court interventions, registration drives, and elected black officials, blacks as a group continue to lag behind whites on most indicators of accomplishment. In some ways, conditions have deteriorated. By contrast, Asians and Indians have made remarkable strides without any electoral empowerment. Like polo, electoral politics may be a worthwhile sport only after first becoming economically successful. How this plunge into electoral politics will play out for today's moral issues—abortion, pornography, religion, sexuality— remains to be seen.

The second lesson is the converse: if domestication is the objective, get the would-be revolutionaries, extremists, grumblers, and malcontents enrolled. Are antigovernment militias posing a problem? Take a clue from the Motor Voter bill and allow voter registration at all firearms and survival equipment stores. Voting, even corrupt voting, should be as convenient as possible. Rig the district boundaries so that leaders must serve their time in state capitals and Washington, D.C., consorting with generous lobbyists. Make those with talent precinct captains, election judges, convention delegates, county commissioners, and paid advisors to established political parties. Within the decade the militiamen will be as threatening as an agitated American Legion post forced to give up its bingo.

In sum, as we observe the 1996 campaign, we should not be distracted by the details. Far more goes on than selecting candidates. Despite the acrimony and divisiveness, all the talk of a people freely exercising sovereignty, we are witnessing a ceremony for reinvigorating the covenant between citizen and state. All sorts of would-be troublemakers are being domesticated and brought into "the system." Those who attempt to escape will be brought to the attention of the Department of Justice.

20

Why I Would Not
Vote Against Hitler

by Wendy McElroy

Liberty *Magazine (Vol. 5, No. 5, May 1996), pp. 46–47. Published by the Liberty Foundation, Box 1181, Port Townsend WA 98368. This article also appeared in* The Voluntaryist *(No. 85, April 1997), pp. 7–8. Wendy McElroy is author of several books. Her most recent ones are* Queen Smith: The Godless Girl *(Amherst NY: Prometheus, 1999) and* Individualist Feminism of the Nineteenth Century *(Jefferson NC: McFarland, 2001).*

At the last Liberty Conference, an intellectual brawl erupted during a panel discussion on terrorism. Since I consider electoral politics the Milque-toast equivalent to terrorism, my opening statement was a condemnation of voting. My arguments were aimed at libertarians who consider themselves anarchists yet jump to their feet in ebullient applause upon hearing that a fellow libertarian wants to be a politician.

In the two raucous hours that ensued, a question was posed: "If you could have cast the deciding vote against Hitler, would you have done so?" I replied, "No, but I would have no moral objection to putting a bullet through his skull." In essence, I adopted a stronger line—a "plumbline," as Benjamin Tucker phrased it—on eliminating the Hitler threat.

I consider such a bullet to be an act of self-defense in a manner that a ballot could never be. A bullet can be narrowly aimed at a deserving target; a ballot attacks innocent third parties who must endure the consequences of the politician I have assisted into a position of power over their lives. Whoever puts a man into a position of unjust power—that is, a position of political power—must share responsibility for every right he violates thereafter.

The question then shifted: "If there had been no other strategies possible, would you have voted against Hitler?" This postulated a fantasy world which canceled out one of the basic realities of existence: the constant presence of alternatives. In essence, the question became, "If the fabric of reality were rewoven into a different pattern, would you still take the same moral stand?" Since my morals are derived from my views about reality, it was not possible for me to answer this question. But my first response was to wonder what I would have been doing for the months and years that led to the momentous dilemma of whether to scratch an X beside Adolf's name. Or did I have no alternatives then either?

I can address only the reality in which I live and, in a world replete with alternatives, I would not vote for or against Hitler. Let me address a more fundamental question: What is the nature of the state? According to Max Weber, a state is an institution that claims a monopoly of force over a geographical area. It is a form of institutionalized power, and the first step in dissecting its essence is to analyze the defining terms "power" and "institution."

Albert Jay Nock wrote of two sorts of power: social and state. By social power, he meant the amount of freedom individuals actually exercise over their lives—that is, the extent to which they can freely make such choices as where and how to live. By state power, he meant the actual amount of control the government exercises over its subjects' lives—that is, the extent to which it determines such choices as where and how people live. There is an inverse and antagonistic relationship between social and state power. One expands only at the expense of the other.

I stress the word "actual" because the power of the state does not rest on its size—the number of laws on the books or the extent of the territory it claims. A state's power rests on social conditions, such as whether people will obey its laws and how many resources it can command to enforce obedience. A key social condition is how legitimate the state is seen to be. For without the veil of legitimate authority, the people will not obey the state, and it will not long command the resources, such as taxes and manpower, that it needs to live.

In other words, freedom does not depend so much on repealing laws as weakening the state's authority. It does not depend—as political strategists expediently claim—on persuading enough people to vote "properly" so that libertarians can occupy seats of political power and roll back legislation. Unfortunately, this process strengthens the institutional framework that produced unjust laws in the first place: it strengthens the structure of state power by accepting its authority as a tool of change. But state authority can never strengthen social power.

This brings up the issue of institutional analysis. People apply the word "institution" to such wide-ranging concepts as "the family," "the free market," "the church," and "the state." An institution is any stable and widely-accepted mechanism for achieving social and political goals. To a great extent, these institutions function independently of the good or bad intentions of those who use them. For example, as long as everyone respects the rules of the free market, it functions as a mechanism of exchange. The same is true of the state. As long as everyone respects its rules—voting, going through state channels, obeying the law—it functions as a mechanism of social control.

F.A. Hayek popularized the notion of *unintended consequences,* observing that conscious acts often produce unforeseen results. This explains why good men who act through bad institutions will produce bad results. Good men acting through the state will strengthen its legitimacy and its institutional framework. They will weaken social power. Ultimately, whether or not they repeal any particular law becomes as irrelevant to producing freedom as their intentions.

So, returning to the question of voting for Hitler: purely for the sake of argument, I'll grant the possibility that I could morally cast a ballot. Yet even then, I would still refuse to vote against him. Why? Because the essential problem is not Hitler, but the institutional framework that allows a Hitler to grasp a monopoly on power. Without the state to back him up and an election to give him legitimized power, Hitler would have been, at most, the leader of some ragged thugs who mugged people in back alleys. Voting for or against Hitler would only strengthen the institutional framework that produced him—a framework that would produce another of his ilk in two seconds.

Killing Hitler does less damage. But it—like voting—is an admission of utter defeat. Resorting to brute force means that all avenues of social power have been destroyed and I have been reduced to adopting the tactics of the state. Under tyranny, such violence might be justified as long as I could avoid harming innocent third parties. In these circumstances, however, voting could not be justified, because there is a third party. No one has the right to place one human being in a position of political power over another. A consistent libertarian can never authorize one human being to tax and control peaceful activities. And the state is no more than the institutionalized embodiment of this authorization.

You cannot help freedom or social power by bowing your head to Leviathan.

21

End of the Mandate

by Gregory Bresiger

The Free Market *(Vol. 16, No. 11, November 1988), pp. 1–3, a newsletter published by The Ludwig Von Mises Institute, Auburn AL. The author writes about the securities industry from Kew Gardens, New York. He can be reached at Phmarlowe@aol.com.*

Big media outlets are ignoring the quiet revolution that is taking place across America. Politicians don't talk too much about it for obvious reasons. This revolution is building incredible momentum. It now threatens the legitimacy of every level of government, the viability of government management of society, and the credibility of career politicians, assuming someone still has any faith in them.

Tens of millions of Americans have stopped voting. No, they're not lazy. No, they're nor irresponsible. No, they are not indifferent or even apathetic. They are quietly protesting a fraudulent system and no longer see any advantage to taking part. They're making a revolution through inaction.

Big media outlets dismiss them as fools. But people who have given up on voting are anything but fools. They're actually sharp people who can see a disguised fraud. They're Americans who are fed up with a government that taxes, regulates, and controls their lives while offering up voting as a means of convincing people they are doing it to themselves.

Mostly, non-voters are Americans who no longer believe that voting, or even the right to vote, amounts to much. They believe that it's a charade, a game they will no longer play. They no longer want to go through the motions of believing things like Bush's "No New Taxes" pledge or Clinton's promise to cut middle-class taxes. These disgruntled former voters have learned that the rules of the game have been fixed by the ruling elites, who shut out popular opinion while piously telling us to vote and saying how much they love democracy.

They say people who don't vote can't complain about the outcome. But they also say that if your candidate didn't win, you can't complain because that's being a sore loser. You also can't complain if the guy you voted for does something you don't like. Hey, you voted for him, didn't you? You can't win. The game is rigged.

Perhaps 1994 was the last gasp of hope the public will ever utter in politics. That year, a new Republican Congress was voted in on the promise to dismantle the regime. The promise sounded vaguely plausible. After all, wasn't Reagan stymied by a Democratic Congress? But here we sit four years later, and government is bigger, richer, and more powerful that ever. With mid-term elections coming up, who can take seriously Newt Gingrich's newest plan to cut taxes?

What this experience underscores is that campaigns are merely the art of manipulating popular opinion to the benefit of the elites. It's now an American tradition that all is forgotten after election day. Hey, if both parties do it, to whom is the voter going to complain?

Hasn't there always been a fair number of people in this republic who declined to pick one band of pirates over another? Yes, and, in fact, it's an American tradition. When the first popular election for president, was held in 1824, the turnout of eligible voters was about 27 percent. This was despite a franchise that frequently restricted voting rights to property holders and heads of households.

In the early nineteenth century, non-participation did not reflect indifference; it reflected the small role that politics played in people's lives. Politicians, even presidents, did not hold the fate of the nation in their hands. In any case, people were not voting on what the laws should be or what the government should do (all that was settled by the Constitution), but on the very narrow question of who should hold a largely powerless office.

As the franchise was expanded throughout the century, and statism grew along with it, voter participation increased. There were suddenly big issues to decide. Would there be a tariff or an income tax? Would the U.S. be one nation or two or more? Would there be a national bank? Would the U.S. enter into foreign military conflicts? With such questions rolling the American electorate, and the appearance of self-government still intact, voter participation increased to 70 and 80 percent.

But that kind of naivete didn't last long. After World War I, and the revelation that big government was being run by a tiny industrial oligarchy, the newly empowered voter developed a new and sophisticated consciousness of his *real* place in the scheme of things. He began to believe that his much ballyhooed power was largely mythical. By 1924, turnout had plummeted to 40 percent from its high at the turn of the century.

After the 1920s, war and depression got people newly interested in politics, so by 1960, turnout was up again to 63 percent of the voting age population. But the promise of government management flopped again, and voting has declined ever since. With the election of 1996, we reached levels alarming for those who vainly try to convince Americans that the system is worthwhile. And the numbers seem to show no signs of reversal. It is a trend of "30 years of progressively dampening interest in American politics," according to Curtis Gans, a veteran observer of voting patterns.

Consider this: In the last presidential election, only 49 percent of the voting age population turned out. That was the lowest presidential voting number since 1924, according to the Center for the Study of the American Electorate. So far this year, about 19.6 percent of the eligible electorate voted in the primaries, which is a drop of about 3 percent from four years ago.

A U.S. Senate candidate in New York, Mark Green, recently moaned that only "one in six registered Democrats" will show up for his party's primary this fall. Mark, your posters may clutter our neighborhoods, but the people aren't falling for the tripe you and the other Democrats (and Republicans) feed a declining number of voters.

Gans said the off-year elections could produce the lowest turnout in American history. The American people are taking a "who cares?" attitude toward whether the GOP retains control of Congress or the Democrats regain it, not because of a sense of powerlessness.

Let's look at that 49 percent of registered voters who turned out in 1996, a presidential election year. Bill Clinton won 49 percent of the votes of those who bothered to show up. That means Clinton was re-elected as president by about 24 percent of Americans 18 years or older. There are military dictators and Teamsters Union presidents who have had a better mandate than that!

It's not only disgust in government and politics that keeps people away. It's also the knowledge—the conviction—that their vote makes effectively no difference. It is one of 100 million, and its value declines by the year. If you have a friend who plans to vote opposite you, you can both stay home.

Why is the vote worth less and less? Dilution of voter power, for one thing. The franchise was once restricted to people who had the strongest stake in liberty. But today, everyone has a right to vote, even people whose only interest is to vote more transfers for themselves. The voting age was lowered so that people who could be drafted to fight foreign wars could also say "yes" to the politicians who were killing them.

Thanks to the advent of the teen vote, we are subjected to MTV's "Rock the Vote" campaigns, with juveniles telling juveniles whom to vote for and why. This reality is demoralizing.

Does the number of voters per office make a difference? Certainly. In the most populous state, California, with nearly 23 million potential voters, only 44 percent showed up to the polls in 1996. However, Alaska, with half a million voters, managed to get 57 percent out to vote; similarly, Montana mustered a 62 percent turnout rate.

If the elites really want to boost turnout, then there's one answer: Make voting a privilege. Make it worth more. But of course doing that would cut into the whole mythology of the modern state, which is that it rules on everyone's behalf, without discriminating for or against anyone or anything. That's democracy. It's also a lie.

The promise of this informal Don't Vote movement is large. Government's small remaining credibility will waste away. Without credibility, there's no legitimacy, and then factors like authority and respect for government in general fall like dominos. There will be no more "mandate." If politicians can't claim it, they can't act on it. Their power to manipulate us is reduced. All to the good.

Then the average person might start to have his consciousness raised about the huge chasm that separates his interests from those of the ruling elite. He might question why the U.S. government takes nearly half his income, regulates huge swatches of the economy, tosses money around the globe with abandon, imposes sanctions on a dozen countries, and starts unwinnable wars. He will realize that mass democracy, and his participation in it, is what allows the political class to claim there is consensus for its rule.

The President and the members of Congress who won in 1996 were elected by a declining minority of American voters. Despite making voting requirements easier and easier over the past 30 years, despite foolish suggestions from some that non-voters be penalized, the supposed problem has become worse.

Politicians refuse to state the obvious: the vast majority of Americans hate politics and have better things to do. They see the present venal system as one in which candidates are reduced to caricatures who play to the lowest common denominator. They insult voters' intelligence with inane ads asking us to trust people we don't know. During the silly election season, the average voter, after reading this barrage of plaudits in brochures, mailings and ads, is all but urged to nominate the candidate for the first opening in the Blessed Trinity.

Meanwhile, more and more Americans will let the political mountebanks on the Potomac know that we are smarter, much smarter than they think. We will ignore their ads. We will hit the mute button when these political hyenas come on the boob tube. We will trash their leaflets, brochures, and other cockamamie concoctions.

We will walk faster when these political gods, accompanied by their well-paid sycophants, deign to put in an appearance on our streets. And, most of all, we will not pay homage to the leviathan the first week in November. Then the "mandate" to plunder the American people will become the stuff of history.

22

The Limits of
Political Action

by Richard Grant

R. W. Grant, The Incredible Bread Machine: A Study of Capitalism, Freedom, and the State *(San Francisco: Fox & Wilkes, 1999, Second Edition), pp. 236–241. The author's website is Quandaryhouse.com.*

Government is force, and politics is the process of deciding who gets to use it on whom. This is not the best way to solve problems.

By and large, the American people live and work in a marketplace of voluntary transactions based on persuasion and cooperative behavior. That is, the shopkeeper cannot force the customer to put down his money; he can only persuade. The politician, however, lives in a different ethical universe where the ultimate currency is not persuasion but force. From this point on, the values are totally different. In the marketplace the person who panders and demagogues and dissembles will probably remain on the lower rungs of success, but in politics the person who panders and demagogues and dissembles will be praised for his political skill and may end up in the White House.

The ethical standards of the professional politician are simply different from those by which the rest of us try to live. Based ultimately on force, politics is an arena in which the least principled will often rise to the top. Perhaps this is why the professional politician is viewed with such contempt by so many Americans.

During each political campaign season a Los Angeles lawyer named Linda Abrams, a Phi Beta Kappa from UCLA, places a sticker on all her personal correspondence urging, "Don't vote—it only encourages them." But her objection goes beyond a mere distaste for the general tackiness of political behavior. "Political control," she explains, "whether applied to education, energy, business or whatever, is the most disruptive single influence in our society today. But the ballot doesn't permit us to oppose the *concept* of political control; all we can do is choose which group is to exercise it. Better to boycott the polls entirely than to sanction such a meaningless process."

Abrams has identifies a basic problem with political action: the voter may choose between ruler A and ruler B, but he cannot choose that there be *no* ruler.

Small wonder that politicians appear to be "all the same." Essentially, they *are* all the same. The ultimate issue is the individual versus the state, but the politician, as confirmed by his oath of office, has already cast his lot with the state. Each would use the state in a different way, but each, with a few honorable exceptions, would use the state, if not for this noble cause then for that one. A Clinton does not reverse a Bush; he merely shifts the emphasis. Administrations may come and go, but the net thrust of political action will always be in the direction of higher and higher levels of government activity. Accordingly, no matter who wins the election the individual loses; only the state gains, nourished every two years by the bewildered affirmation of the voter.

The divisive nature of political action. The political process creates more problems that it solves. Consider again the contrast between the political and the marketplace transaction. When the shopkeeper sells his product to the customer, each party enjoys a net gain. The shopkeeper values the customer's money more highly than the item (otherwise, he would not sell). The customer, on the other hand, values the item more highly than the money (otherwise, he would not buy). In any voluntary transaction *both* parties experience a net gain. Government action, however, is quite a different matter, for government can give to some only what it has first taken forcibly from others. Unlike the free-market, for every beneficiary of government action there is a victim. Accordingly, government "compassion" will inevitably set group against group.

The divisive nature of political action is most obvious, of course, during a political campaign, with its rampant appeal to bloc voting. Where the marketplace brings people together in mutually profitable exchange, political action drives them apart. The politician must emphasize differences, not common ground. He must stress the advantages which he can gain for this or that group—thus arousing the resentment of the rest who know quite well that it will be taken out of *their* hides, one way or another. The rich resent the poor because of welfare; the poor resent the rich because of fat government contracts and subsidies. Whites resent blacks because of affirmative action, while blacks resent whites because of white values forced upon them in white-dominated public schools. Farmers resent subsidized aerospace engineers, while aerospace engineers resent subsidized farmers, and on and on. Political action does not resolve these antagonisms—it causes them.

The extent to which diverse races and cultures and interests are able to live together in relative harmony is the extent to which each poses no threat to the other. When life is dominated by government, however, each faction in its own defense is turned against the rest. In Northern Ireland, for example, because housing, education, jobs, money, health care, etc., are all controlled by the state, Catholics must struggle for political power— and fearful Protestants must struggle to prevent them from getting it. In his book *The Economics and Politics of Race,* Thomas Sowell notes the dangers inherent in the politically-run society.

> The politicization of economic and social life increases the costs of intergroup differences, and tends to heighten mutual hostility.... Politics offers "free" benefits for people to fight over. Markets put prices on benefits, forcing each group to limit its own use of them, thereby in effect sharing with others. A society with both Buddhist and Islamic citizens must somehow allocate its available building materials in such a way as to have these materials shared in the building of temples and mosques. If the building materials are shared through economic processes, each set of religious followers weighs costs against benefits and limits its demand accordingly. But if these same building materials are provided free or are otherwise shared through political processes, each group has an incentive to demand the lion's share—or all—of the materials for building its own place of worship, which is always more urgently needed, in more grandiose proportions, than the other.
>
> Groups that hate each other often transact peacefully in the market place but erupt into violence when their conflicting interests are at stake in political decisions.[1]

Wherever one looks, the principle is the same: political control aggravates every difference, heightens every suspicion and intensifies every hatred. The greatest generator of social discord is government—the institution of legalized force. Only in a free-market, non-political society can the spirit of live-and-let-live prevail.

The myth of political reform. The state is force. Nothing else. Not persuasion or cooperation or brotherhood; just force. But an institution based on force will be virtually immune to reform.

---

[1] *Thomas Sowell,* The Economics and Politics of Race *(New York: William Morrow and Company, Inc., 1983), p. 246.*

The political mechanism will work inexorably to the advantage of those who seek the favors of the state, and to the disadvantage of those who pay the ever-mounting bill. For example, consider the unequal contest over (let us say) a proposed subsidy for this or that industry.

Because those in favor of the proposal have much at stake, their lobbying efforts will be intensive and well-financed. To the individual taxpayer, however, the impact will be at most a few pennies per year. Accordingly, opposition will be muted and dispersed. Only on April 15 will the accumulated impact of such handouts be brought to the attention of the victimized taxpayer. Yet, even then (especially then!) he has no real choice in the matter: he must pay or go to jail. And so, year by year and decade by decade, the handouts multiply in number and the tax burden builds higher and higher. The political process is not a means of solving this problem; based on force, the political process *is* the problem.

Imposed ultimately by the tax collector and the jail cell, the beneficiaries of government largess are insulated from the counterbalances by which the rest of us are automatically restrained. For example, the businessman might indeed wish to raise his prices again and again, but he is limited ultimately by the willingness of the customer to buy his product. The laborer would be equally glad to receive a thousand dollars an hour for his efforts, but he too is limited by the willingness of others to support his desires. Government, however, based on force, is undeterred by "consumer resistance." Because the out-voted taxpayer must pay his taxes or go to jail, those on the receiving end of government "compassion" can vote for more and more of the same without limit. The long-term danger is obvious.

> A democracy ... can only exist until the voters discover they can vote themselves largess out of the public treasury. From that moment on the majority always votes for the candidate promising the most benefits from the public treasury with the result that Democracy always collapses over a loose fiscal policy, always to be followed by a Dictatorship.[2]

Does this sound as though it might apply today? This statement was written 200 years go by Professor Alexander Fraser Tytler as he described the collapse of the Athenian Republic over 2000 years before.

The interests of the politician and of the private citizen conflict not only in means but in ends. The private citizen (at least the one who is not himself the beneficiary of government favor) seeks minimum interference

---

[2] *Cited in* The Freeman, *date unknown.*

with his life, but the politician has good reason to push in precisely the opposite direction—being human, he does not pursue insignificance; like the rest of us, he seeks a measure of importance, prestige and influence. His interests then, are not served by minimizing the role of government, but by maximizing the role of the institution of which he is a part.

To seek reform by political means, then, is an exercise in futility. This or that scoundrel might be turned out of office, but a fundamental change in direction is unlikely. Based on force, the relentless state is inherently immune to reform—at least from within.

The myth of majority rule. The state is force, and politics is simply the means of determining who is in charge; the game of deciding who coerces whom for whose benefit. In itself, this is not a productive process. But another reason government seems so strangely, congenitally incapable of running things sensibly arises from the very nature of representative government.

We do not wish an *un*representative government, of course. So we try very hard to make it as representative as possible. Hence the ultimate political ideal of majority rule. But here the problem emerges, for where an issue is in doubt, *the majority is always wrong*. Consider that any major break-through in the understanding of things will *always* be greeted with indifference or opposition by the majority. (Otherwise it would not be a breakthrough at all, but an already accepted truth!) When Copernicus suggested that the earth went around the sun, the majority believed otherwise. When private individuals in eighteenth century England introduced the "barbaric" practice of inoculating against smallpox, the majority, including virtually the entire medical profession, was appalled. The majority laughed at the Wright Brothers and ignored Bell. A breakthrough, by definition, concerns something previously undiscovered and unaccepted. Advances are then made by individuals or by small groups of cooperating people who *overcome* majority opinion or indifference. Later, of course, when the innovators are finally proven right, the majority comes along. At the outset, however, when the issue is in doubt, the majority is always wrong.

The fact that the majority is always wrong has interesting implications for the concept of democracy—a system which, to many, means state control of the individual and his property in accordance with the supposed wishes of the majority. But if the majority is invariably wrong, how fare those areas under state domination? Science? Industry? The arts? Clearly, the thrust of any state-directed effort, in accordance with majority rule, will always be in the direction of the safe, the sure, the average, the uninspired, the mediocre. What does this mean, then, to our treasured concept of "progress" via political means? It means that any "progress" which comes about through political action will not be progress at all; it will be either a prevention of something better or a regression to something worse. In a word, where majority rules, progress stops.

And so one is drawn to the conclusion that majority rule is a false god; that the goal of free people should not be majority rule at all but self-rule, not political action but individual action, not the "public interest" but private interest. The Bill of Rights does not tell the majority what it *may* do, but what it may *not* do. When the individual is free to pursue his own self-interest (limited only by the equal right of others to do the same), the public weal will take care of itself.

The limits of political action. Government is force, and politics is simply the means of deciding who gets to use it at whose expense. By its nature, then, politics will inexorably represent the interests of those who seek the favors of government. Hence the bewilderment of voters who find that no matter who wins the election, government continues to grow bigger and more intrusive. At best, transient reforms can be accomplished, but the underlying dynamic of politics is constantly to expand the role of the state.

Accordingly, those seeking to limit the role of political force in our society are quite literally disenfranchised. Linda Abrams was mostly right: you can vote for ruler A or ruler B, but you can't vote for *no* ruler. Political action can possibly be helpful for educational purposes, or as a rearguard effort, but its effectiveness as an influence for less government is limited. It is simply the wrong instrument.

So, is history implacably against us? Is Tytler's grim scenario written in our stars?

History does not make people; people make history, and they can change its course when they choose to do so. In fact, people have within their grasp a weapon far more effective than the ballot: they have the ability to say "no"—to withhold the sanction without which government is powerless. Attitudes are changing, and that sanction is gradually being withdrawn as people turn away from government and toward the voluntary alternatives of the marketplace. Political government as we know it may already be in its twilight.

23

Why I Refuse to Register (to Vote or Pay Taxes)

Anonymous

Anonymous, The Voluntaryist *(No. 100, October 1999), p. 2.*

To the Editor of *The Voluntaryist,*

I am anonymously sending this letter to you after looking at *The Voluntaryist* website while surfing the Internet (http://members.aol.com/vlntryist). It appears that my ideas might fit somehow with what you call voluntaryism.

I am one of the tens of millions of Americans who don't file tax returns or voluntarily pay taxes. I'm writing this letter to explain something that you and your readers may not be aware of. The reasons for not filing tax returns or voluntarily paying taxes, and not voting, are similar.

They are similar in that both taxes and voting are activities that demand involvement with that coercive institution known as government. Government exercises a monopoly of legal control over a certain geographic area. This encompasses coercive monopolization of the major services that it provides us. To fund these services, the government unilaterally imposes a compulsory levy upon us. These "taxes" are not based on the amount of service the government provides us, nor upon our request for them. (The government does not offer us the opportunity to do without a particular service, or shop elsewhere for it, or to negotiate the price.) It doesn't care if we didn't want the service, didn't use all that was offered, or simply refused it altogether. The government declares it a crime if we refuse to pay all or part of "our share." It attempts to punish this refusal by making us serve time in jail or confiscating some of our property, or both.

The main reason, however, why I refuse to pay taxes is that I don't want to give my sanction to the government. I, for one, do not consent to our particular government, nor do I want to support any coercive institution. I object, on principle, to the forced collection of taxes because *taxes are a euphemism for *stealing*. (By stealing, I mean taking another person's property without his voluntary consent.) Stealing is not an activity that leads to social harmony or prosperity. Stealing is anti-life. It is not an activity that can be universalized. If it were, it would result in death and destruction for all. Furthermore, "stealing" or "taxation" is wasteful. Everyone agrees that government money is spent unwisely, wastefully, and on at least some project(s) which would not be voluntarily supported by some taxpayers. But, even if the spending were not wasteful or for some improper purpose, I would still object strenuously because taxes are theft. In other words, I object to the means (the compulsion used by the government)— regardless of how efficiently the money is spent or what it is spent on. I do not want it said about me that I cooperated with the government.

Similarly, I refuse to participate in the electoral process (I simply refuse to register to vote) because I do not want it ever said that I supported the state. When you play a game, you agree to abide by the rules and accept the outcome. Well, I simply refuse to play, and in clear conscience can say that I am not bound by the outcome. Furthermore, there [are] many reprehensible activities taken by the government (you choose your own example) which I do not wish to support. Governments need legitimacy, and one of the major means of establishing legitimacy is to claim that the voters support the government. Just imagine if everyone refused to vote and pay taxes. Government would shrivel up. But, before that happened legislators at every level would probably pass laws that would make voting compulsory. This has already happened in some countries.

I recently read an article by Charles Reich (from his column, "Reflections," on "The Limits of Duty") that appeared in the June 19, 1971, issue of *The New Yorker*. It was written during the Vietnam era, when many draft-age college students were resisting conscription into the United States military forces. Reich wrote:

> Perhaps the best way to understand those who have resisted the draft—by seeking conscientious-objector status, by going to jail, by fleeing to Canada—is to acknowledge that they are demanding to live and to be judged by the old standards as fully responsible moral beings. They are seeking law, not evading it. Finding no acceptable standard of conduct available in today's organizational society, they have gone to standards that are not their own personal fiat but the old, traditional standards of religion, ethics, and common law. They are saying that they refuse to act in a

way that common experience tells them will produce evil—evil that we know about or should know about [emphasis added, p. 55].

In other words, in refusing to register to vote and in refusing to "register" to pay taxes, I am going back to "the old, traditional standards of religion, ethics, common law," and common sense. I am refusing to act in a way that produces or contributes to evil. I rest my case.

24

Non-Voting as an
Act of Secession

by Hans Sherrer

This is an unpublished piece specially prepared for this anthology. The author is an independent businessman in Portland, Oregon.

In 1776, the Declaration of Independence made it plain that in America, "Governments are instituted among Men, deriving their just powers from the consent of the governed,—That whenever any Form of Government becomes destructive..., it is the Right of the People to alter or abolish it,..." The consent theory stated by the Declaration is standard fare in American politics. The Declaration, however, failed to address a very important question: How do individuals express their disapproval of a political regime and/or withdraw their consent from a government that they deem "destructive?"

There are several methods that Americans have used to demonstrate their lack of consent. One way is to renounce allegiance to an existing political order. The colonists in North America seceded from the British empire by successfully waging the Revolutionary War. On the other hand, the eleven Confederate states removed themselves from the federal union from 1861 to 1865, before being forcibly reintegrated back into the United States.[1]

A second way someone can express a lack of consent is to move to a different country. This is what several commentators have called "the exit

---

[1]*It should be noted that the Confederate States successfully seceded, and that each state had to reapply for admission to the United States. The States were occupied by federal troops in order to coerce them into complying with these conditions. If the use of coercion to obtain their "consent" was illegal and immoral (as it would be in obtaining a signature on an ordinary contract), then what does this say about the status of these states today?*

option."[2] History teaches that the last resort of the individual against tyranny is to escape from its jurisdiction. The Jews left Egypt; the Separatists fled England. History is replete with examples of people who "voted with their feet."

A third way people express a lack of consent is by *not voting*. Although political pundits might not call it a withdrawal of consent, the fact is that millions upon millions of Americans show their displeasure with their government by not registering for and/or casting a ballot in political elections. Non-voting represents an exit from political society. It is a silent form of "social power" that speaks volumes. Choosing not to vote may be a form of apathy, but it is simultaneously an expression of "what I perceive is best for me."

In other words, millions of non-voters are implicitly stating that voting is a meaningless and unimportant activity, so far as it applies to them and their loved ones in their own lives. After all, government programs, and spending and tax policies will continue regardless of how anyone votes. Furthermore, for those thinking individuals who understand that the government must "get out the vote," the choice *not to vote* is a form of personal empowerment and a psychologically life-affirming act.[3] Those men and women who consciously choose *not* to participate in politics expose the lie behind the myth of "government by consent." They have not consented to anything. In other words, their decision *not to vote* is a form of personal secession—the form of secession that is most readily available to them.[4]

This choice is exercised by many millions of Americans because they understand that elections are nothing more than tugs-of-war between tweedledum Democrats and tweedledee Republicans. Both parties seek the mantle of power to impose their agendas on society. Politicians of every political party want to continue the flow of tax money into the treasury and to pass laws allowing the government to increasingly invade the social spheres of daily life. As social commentator, one-time political candidate, and author Gore Vidal once noted: there is really only one political party in this country, and it has *two* incestuously related branches.[5]

Whether based on intuition or practical understanding, non-voters

---

[2] *See Albert O. Hirschman,* Exit, Voice, and Loyalty: Responses to Decline in Firms, Organizations, and States, *Cambridge: Harvard University Press, 1970.*

[3] *See "Remarks on the Psychological Aspects of Totalitarianism," in Bruno Bettelheim,* Surviving and Other Essays, *New York: Vintage Books, 1980, pp. 317–332.*

[4] *Carl Watner, editor of this anthology, first suggested this concept to me.*

[5] *See "Homage to Daniel Shays," in Gore Vidal,* Homage to Daniel Shays: Collected Essays 1952–1972, *New York: Random House, 1972, pp. 434–449.*

realize they only have a subservient role in the political structure described by Vidal. Without money, position or connections, they are disenfranchised from having any meaningful say-so in the government's impact on their lives. Yet, in spite of this handicap, choosing *not to vote* can have a dramatic and positive effect on society. This is because a government's survival is dependent on having a sufficient number of people grant it the appearance of legitimacy to act and elicit obedience.[6]

Whether it is an explicit intention or an implicit result, the decision not to vote is a way of decreasing governmental legitimacy. As Vladimir Bukovsky, the Russian dissident put it: "Power rests on nothing other than people's consent to submit, and each person who refuses to submit to tyranny reduces it by one two-hundred-and-fifty-millionth, whereas each who compromises [with it] only increases it."[7] Finally, there reaches a point at which a government no longer has enough consensus to act under any authority other than the exercise of raw, naked power. Once the mirage of legitimacy is gone, a government must become openly despotic to remain in power. This, in turn, tends to turn even more people away from supporting it, and can put its continued existence in doubt.

This isn't armchair speculation. History records that variations of this scenario have occurred numerous times.[8] Who would have predicted that the Marco regime would fall from power in the Philippines? Who ever expected that the Communist government in Poland would be succeeded by Solidarity? Who ever thought that the Union of Soviet Socialist Republics would "splinter apart" in what seemed like the blink of an eye? However, it is usually a surprise to the "experts" when it happens, because it occurs quickly and at a time when a State appears, from the outside, to be at the height of its power.

This phenomenon of seemingly sudden social change is explained by physicist Per Bak's theory of *self-organizing criticality*.[9] This theory, for example, explains how millions of grains of sand can methodically be added to a seemingly stable sand pile until a "point of criticality" is

---

[6] See Herbert C. Kelman and V. Lee Hamilton, Crimes of Obedience: Toward a Social Psychology of Authority and Responsibility, *New Haven: Yale University Press, 1989, p. 116.*

[7] Vladimir Bukovsky, To Build a Castle—My Life as a Dissenter, *New York: The Viking Press, 1977, p. 240.*

[8] See Kenneth E. Boulding, "The Impact of the Draft on the Legitimacy of the National State," in Sol Tax (ed.), The Draft, *Chicago: University of Chicago Press, 1967, pp. 191–196. Also see Joseph A. Tainter,* The Collapse of Complex Societies, *Cambridge: Cambridge University Press, 1997 (reprint edition).*

[9] Per Bak, How Nature Works: The Science of Self-Organized Criticality, *New York: Springer-Verlag, 1996.*

reached. At that point, adding only one more grain of sand will trigger an avalanche. Professor Bak's theory has been used to help understand such diverse things as traffic flow and the trading of stocks. It is equally applicable to the delegitimizing impact *any one* non-voter can have on a political regime.

It is within the realm of possibility that some day the illegitimacy of the government of the United States might reach the point of criticality. What would happen if impassioned non-voters used the many methods of modern communications to express their ideas and dissatisfaction to others? At first thought it might seem preposterous to seriously consider that government in the United States could become delegitimized. It isn't. As sociologist Sebastian Scheerer has observed: "[T]here has never been a major social transformation in the history of mankind that ha[s] not been looked upon as unrealistic, idiotic, or utopian by the large majority of experts even a few years before the unthinkable became reality."[10]

For a variety of reasons which the French author, Jacques Ellul, outlined in his book, *The Political Illusion*, non-voters choose to dispel the myth that the voters control the political process.[11] Instead of debasing themselves and dignifying the elections that have no positive impact on their lives, over a hundred million Americans regularly choose to distance themselves from the voting process and the political regime legitimized by it. They do so by selecting the option of *not voting*. The non-voters are right, and they are winning every election held in America.

---

[10] *Sebastian Scheerer, "Towards Abolitionism," in* Contemporary Crises, *Vol. 10, p. 7; quoted in* Thomas Mathiesen, Prison on Trial: A Critical Assessment, *Thousand Oaks: SAGE Publications, 1990, p. 156.*

[11] *Jacques Ellul, translated by Konrad Kellen,* The Political Illusion, *New York: Alfred A. Knopf, 1967.*

25

Laconics: Short Takes on Non-Voting

No matter who gets elected, the government always gets in.

When you undertake political action and support a candidate, and your guy wins, it means that instead of being sold out by someone you opposed, you will be betrayed by someone you supported.—Ron Neff

An honest politician is as unthinkable as an honest burglar.—H.L. Mencken

With all respect to differences among types of government, there is not, in strict theory, any difference between the powers available to the democratic and to the totalitarian state.—Robert Nisbet

If you injected truth into politics, you'd have no politics.—Will Rogers

When it comes to government power, there are no good men.—Robert LeFevre

Participation is an instrument of conquest because it encourages people to give their consent to being governed.... Deeply imbedded in people's sense of fair plays is the principle that those who play the game must accept the outcome. Those who participate in politics are similarly committed, even if they are consistently on the losing side. Why do politicians plead with everyone to get out and vote? Because voting is the simplest and easiest form of participation by masses of people. Even though it is minimal participation, it is sufficient to commit all voters to being governed, regardless of who wins.—Theodore Lowi, *Incomplete Conquest*, New York: Holt, Rhinehart & Winston, 1981, pp. 25–26.

The decisive means for politics is violence.... Anyone who fails to see this is, indeed, a political infant.—Max Weber, 75 *American Political Science Review* (1981), p. 901.

Democracy is essentially coercive. The winners get to use public authority to impose their policies on the losers.—John E. Chubb and Terry M. Moe, *Politics, Markets, and American Schools*, Washington, D.C.: Brookings Institution, 1990, p. 28.

I never vote, It only encourages the politicians.

If voting could change things it would be illegal.

One is a lie, two are lies, three are politics.—an old Jewish proverb.

Epilogue: "Reasons to Vote"

by John Roscoe and Ned Roscoe

Bagatorials *(New York: A Fireside Book published by Simon & Schuster, 1996), p. 16.*

1. Get off work early.
2. Get out of doing tasks for spouse.
3. Your parents told you to vote.
4. Protect your patronage job.
5. To avoid feeling guilty.
6. Your spouse nags you to vote.
7. Your employer pressures you to vote.
8. You get a monetary gain from the results.
9. Television tells you to vote.
10. You dislike someone so much you vote for his or her opponent.
11. You worry about what will happen to society if you don't vote.
12. It shows you have an opinion.
13. If you couldn't vote, you'd be outraged.
14. You want to show you speak English.
15. You can meet friends and neighbors at the polling place and discuss affairs and do business.
16. Walking a mile to the polls is good for your health.
17. One can announce to friends smugly, "I've already voted."
18. You may meet Elvis at the polls.

Index